HANDS ON GRAMMAR

Multimodal Grammar and Language Mini Lessons
Grades 4-9
2nd Edition

Katherine S. McKnight, Ph.D.

Copyright © 2021
Katherine S. McKnight, Ph.D.

All rights reserved. No part of this book may be reproduced
in any form or by an electronic or mechanical means, including
information storage and retrieval systems, without permission
in writing from the publisher, except by reviewers, who may quote brief
passages in review.

Edited by Elaine Carlson
Front Cover design, layout and additional graphics by Sydney Lawson
and Kris Lantzy

Published by Engaging Learners, LLC
Antioch, IL

Visit KatherineMcKnight.com

For Ellie and Colin, my children, who teach me
lessons everyday and bring joy to my life;

For David, my husband and best friend, who
encourages me to dream.

ACKNOWLEDGMENTS

With all projects like writing a book, there are numerous people to thank and recognize. I would like to thank the many teachers who graciously allowed me to access their classrooms to co-teach, observe, and problem solve as we worked together to ensure that all children are engaged in dynamic and powerful learning.

Elaine Carlson, the goddess of all things administrative is integral in all aspects of my professional work, including this book. If you call the Engaging Learners office, her pleasant demeanor is always on the other line. Sydney Lawson and Kris Lantzy designed the cover, layout, graphics, and illustrations. I am lucky to know so many talented professionals.

QR CODES

This book uses QR codes, which are scannable codes that let you easily access a website. You can scan them using the camera app on your phone. When you point the camera at the QR code, it will automatically scan it, so there's no need to take a photo! After the camera scans the code, you will receive a notification at the top of the screen. Once you click on the notification bar, you will be taken to the website.

1. Scan the QR code in the camera app

2. Click on the notifcation

ABOUT THE AUTHOR

Dr. Katherine McKnight is a dynamic presenter, dedicated teacher, and award-winning author. She began her career in education over 30 years ago as a middle school and high school English and social studies teacher in the Chicago Public Schools. In addition to speaking at professional development conferences, she is a regular consultant in schools and classrooms in the United States and internationally.

Dr. McKnight has served as a Distinguished Professor of Research at National Louis University. She is the founder of Engaging Learners, an educational company built around her successful Literacy & Learning Center model. Her work in educational leadership, literacy and student skill development has resulted in unprecedented academic achievement in many struggling schools.

Katie has received several awards for her publications and teaching at the university level. She has authored 20 books that support educational strategies to engage all learners. Her titles include the best-selling *The Teacher's Big Book of Graphic Organizers*, winner of the 2013 Teachers' Choice Award. She's also written *The Second City Guide to Improv in the Classroom*, *Teaching Writing in the Inclusive Classroom*, *The Teacher's Big Book of Graphic Organizers: 100 Reproducible Organizers that Help Kids with Reading, Writing, and the Content Areas*, *Literacy and Learning Centers for the Big Kids: Building Literacy Skills and Content Knowledge* and *Strategies to Support Struggling Adolescent Readers*.

For more classroom resources, visit her website at KatherineMcKnight.com!

TABLE OF CONTENTS

Lesson 1	Action Contractions	12
Lesson 2	Adjectives Abound	16
Lesson 3	Adjectives Carousel	20
Lesson 4	Apostrophes in Public	24
Lesson 5	Applicable Appositive	30
Lesson 6	The Colon	34
Lesson 7	Commas - An Overview	38
Lesson 8	Commas, Part Two	42
Lesson 9	Comma Match	46
Lesson 10	Common Nouns	50
Lesson 11	Connecting Clauses	54
Lesson 12	Dependent Clauses	58
Lesson 13	End Punctuation Marks	62
Lesson 14	Fragments and Run-Ons	68
Lesson 15	Further vs. Farther	72
Lesson 16	Homonyms	76
Lesson 17	Hyphens	82
Lesson 18	Idiomatic Expressions, Part One	86
Lesson 19	Idiomatic Expressions, Part Two	90
Lesson 20	Its and It's	94

TABLE OF CONTENTS

Lesson 21	Metaphorical Expressions	98
Lesson 22	Modifiers are Dangling	102
Lesson 23	Onomatopoeia	106
Lesson 24	Placing Prepositions	110
Lesson 25	Prefix Carousel	114
Lesson 26	Prefix Puzzle	118
Lesson 27	Pronoun Practice	122
Lesson 28	Pronouns: Gender Impact	126
Lesson 29	Pronouns: Possessive	132
Lesson 30	Proper Nouns	136
Lesson 31	Quotation Marks, Part One	140
Lesson 32	Quotation Marks, Part Two	144
Lesson 33	Semicolon	148
Lesson 34	Sentence Fragments	154
Lesson 35	Spelling Words that Challenge Us	158
Lesson 36	Subject and Verb Agreement	165
Lesson 37	Writer's Proofreading Checklist	168
Lesson 38	Very	174
Lesson 39	Words that are Confusing	180
Lesson 40	Your and You're	184

FIGURE INDEX

1.1	Word + Word = Contraction	14
1.2	Puzzle Piece Example	14
1.3	Puzzle Piece Templates	15
2.1	Student Sample: Adjectives Abound	18
2.2	Adjectives Abound Handout	19
3.1	Student Sample: Adjectives Carousel	22
3.2	Adjectives Carousel Handout	23
4.1	Student Sample: Apostrophes in Public	27
4.2	Apostrophes in Public Graphic Organizer	28
5.1	Student Sample: Applicable Appositives	32
5.2	Applicable Appositive Handout	33
6.1	Colon Lesson Example	37
7.1	Ten Quick Comma Rules Handout	41
8.1	Ten Commas Activity Materials	44
8.2	Five More Comma Rules Handout	45
9.1	Comma Rules Activity Materials	49
9.2	Comma Rules Examples Activity Materials	49
11.1	Clause Rules Activity Example	56
11.2	Clause Rules Handout	57
12.1	Materials for Lesson Twelve	60
13.1	Materials for Lesson Thirteen	65
14.1	Materials for Lesson Fourteen	71
16.1	Common Homonyms Handout	79
16.2	Student Sample: Homonym Tableaux	80
16.3	Homonym Tableaux Planning Sheet	81
17.1	Student Sample: Homonym Poster	85
18.1	Idiomatic Expressions Graphic Organizer	89

FIGURE INDEX

19.1	Idiomatic Expressions: Part Two Graphic Organizer	93
20.1	Its and It's Worksheet	97
21.1	Student Sample: Metaphorical Expressions	100
21.2	Metaphorical Expressions Handout	101
22.1	Practicing Correcting Sentences with Dangling Modifiers Handout	104
22.2	Dangling Modifiers: Suggested Revisions	105
24.1	List of Common Prepositions	113
25.1	Prefix Carousel Activity Example	116
25.2	Commonly Used Prepositions	117
26.1	Prefix Graphic Organizer	121
27.1	Pronoun Practice Handout	125
28.1	Student Sample: Pronouns - Gender Impact	129
28.2	Pronouns - Gender Impact Handout	130
28.3	Pronouns - Gender Impact Graphic Organizer	131
30.1	Proper Nouns Handout	139
33.1	Semicolons Graphic Organizer	152
34.1	Sentence Fragment Strips	157
35.1	Words That Are Tricky to Spell Handout	161
35.2	Student Sample: Personal Spelling Dictionary	162
35.3	Personal Spelling Dictionary Graphic Organizer	163
37.1	Writer's Proofreading Handout	171
37.2	Proofreading Practice Slips	172
37.3	Writer's Proofreading Checklist	173
38.1	Very - Synonym Worksheet Slips	177
38.2	Very Handout	178
39.1	Confusing Word Pairs Handout	183
40.1	Your Bananas / You're Bananas Activity Materials	187

ABOUT THIS BOOK

I have always been intimidated by grammar. It was hard enough to use, let alone teach! Like so many other teachers, I learned grammar from big books that stated important definitions like, "a noun is a person, place, thing, or idea" and "a verb is an action word." As a high school student, I struggled to learn how to apply these definitions to multiple-choice assessments. Most of the time it didn't make sense to me. My teachers would say things like, "You have to learn grammar for college and to be a better writer." While I certainly don't disagree with my teachers' advice all those years ago, I do disagree with their methods. Learning grammar from a book and applying it on multiple-choice worksheets didn't make me a better writer. I actually became a more tense and frightened writer. I was afraid I'd forget something or make stupid mistakes. As I progressed through my teacher preparation program after graduating with a Bachelor of Arts in American Civilization, I learned that my high school experience wasn't unique. It turns out that for the vast majority of students, learning grammar in isolation doesn't work. Instead, evidence shows that grammar and writing mechanics are best taught within the context of writing.

When I was a newly minted high school teacher myself, I valiantly tried to teach my students to use grammar knowledge to become better writers. I gobbled up advice from Nancie Atwell and Linda Reif. I had some success, but I struggled to get my students' understanding of grammatical 'rules' to correlate with the texts they composed. I knew that I was screwing it up and needed to find some way to help them make the connection between more abstract grammatical concepts and more concrete writing experiences. Where would I find a solution to my teaching turmoil? Little did I know, the solution would be found in my math teacher colleagues' teaching.

Oftentimes, math teachers use physical models to demonstrate and explain abstract concepts. I wondered if I could do the same to teach grammar. Like math, grammar is abstract for most adolescents. I started to explore manipulatives for the teaching of grammar and I looked to Howard Gardner's theory of multiple intelligences for inspiration. As I tinkered with these models, I saw a change in my students. Learning about apostrophes, subject/verb agreement, and proper nouns became exciting and tangible. During this period of discovery, my students and I began to understand that learning about grammar was actually about learning how to manipulate and use language to become more effective writers.

As I learned how to develop grammar and writing lesson that actively involve multiple intelligences, I noticed that my students were better internalizing what I was teaching. I had far greater success in teaching students about grammar and writing than I did using worksheets and grammar books.

This second edition is slight revision of the original, 2011, edition. The new graphics and updated styling help make the book more organized and easier to read.

HOW TO USE THIS BOOK

This book contains forty grammar and language mini lessons that incorporate kinesthetic models and Gardner's theory of multiple intelligences. As you look through the lessons and consider which ones to use with your students, there are a few things to remember and know.

Determine Content Need: If seventh-grade students need to learn how to use commas, it might be appropriate to teach each of the ten comma rules in a series of ten separate mini lessons. When teaching the comma rules to twelfth-graders, however, we would hope that all of rules could be covered in one mini lesson that reviews this material.

Keep Them Short: The whole point of grammar mini lessons is to break down concepts into small, digestible chunks. Any mini lesson that is more than ten minutes in length is too long. If you have a mini lesson that is ten minutes or more, it is time to review the content and revise.

Make Them Simple: Mini lessons are most effective when the grammar or writing concept is the smallest digestible chunk. Covering common nouns, proper nouns, and collective nouns in one lesson may be too much. Cover each type of noun in a separate mini lesson.

Engage Students and Provide for Interaction: Our students have access to almost unlimited information at their fingertips, so our classrooms have to be more than just places to transmit facts. The most effective classrooms provide interesting, hands-on, instructional experiences that give students a chance to practice "real world" applications.

Provide Practice Time: Before students are ready to transfer what they learn about grammar and writing into their personal writing, they need practice. In general, follow this structure. Phase 1: teach the concept; Phase 2: allow for practice; and Phase 3: (which is the most important) students apply the concept to their individual writing.

Consider What's Next: If the students understand common nouns, proper nouns, and collective nouns, it is probably time to teach about apostrophes, or adjectives.

Evaluate: The best way to assess whether the students understand the grammatical and writing concepts that were taught is to determine whether the students have applied them to their writing. Writing rubrics or checklists, that list the successful application of grammatical and writing concepts, will help you to monitor individual mastery. As with all classroom activities, it is extremely helpful for all of the students when you provide both verbal and written directions. Written directions can be on a sheet of paper, on poster board, or simply written on the whiteboard or displayed overhead.

Lesson 1

Action Contractions

Overview and Tips for Classroom Implementation

Students, especially English Language Learners (ELL), often do not understand that the apostrophe mark in a contraction like "can't" or "wouldn't" actually signals to the reader that there are letters missing. In this activity the students pair puzzle pieces to create contractions. I often taught this mini lesson at the beginning of class.

Lesson Instructions

First, photocopy the Puzzle Piece Templates (Figure 1.3). Write a contraction on one puzzle piece and write the words that make up the contraction on a matching piece. Refer to the table (Figure 1.1) as a resource. Option: instead of using the template, use index cards or recycle a cardboard jigsaw puzzle by writing on the back.

Next, distribute one puzzle piece per student. Once the students have a puzzle piece, instruct the them to find the matching puzzle piece.

Then, once the students are correctly paired, have them create a single line or a circle so that they can see all of the contractions. Discuss the different contractions with the students.

Skills Covered in this Lesson

- Demonstrate command of the conventions of standard English grammar and usage when writing or speaking.
- Demonstrate command of the conventions of standard English capitalization, punctuation and spelling when writing.

Teacher Tip!

When I conduct this mini lesson in the classroom, I use it as an opening activity. When students enter the classroom at the beginning of the class period, I hand them a puzzle piece. While I take attendance, the students find their contraction pair and line up. It is helpful to create the puzzle pieces on matching color paper. It allows the students to do a quick check to ensure that their contraction is correct.

Word + Word = Contraction

is + not = isn't	did + not = didn't	you + would = you'd
are + not = aren't	can + not = can't	you + have = you've
was + not = wasn't	could + not = couldn't	he + is = he's
were + not = weren't	should + not = shouldn't	he + will = he'll
have + not = haven't	might + not = mightn't	he + would = he'd
has + not = hasn't	must + not = mustn't	he + has = he's
had + not = hadn't	I + am = I'm	she + is = she's
will + not = won't	I + will = I'll	she + will = she'll
would + not = wouldn't	I + had = I'd	she + would = she'd
do + not = don't	you + are = you're	she + has = she's
does + not = doesn't	you + will = you'll	she + had = she'd

Figure 1.1

Figure 1.2

Puzzle Piece Templates

Figure 1.3

Lesson Two

Adjectives Abound

Overview and Tips for Classroom Implementation

Adding descriptive language in student writing can be challenging. This mini lesson utilizes strong visuals to prompt students to use adjectives and to develop skills for incorporating figurative language in narrative writing.

Lesson Instructions

First, collect pictures from different kinds of sources. Allow the students to work in pairs for this mini lesson. The students can select pictures from your collection.

Next, instruct the students to record all of the adjectives that they could use to describe the selected picture. Give the students three minutes to complete the list. It's helpful to display a timer.

Then, once the students have completed the list, instruct them to use a thesaurus to add to the list.

Finally, using the adjective list, the student pairs write a narrative paragraph about the picture.

Skills Covered in this Lesson

- Use knowledge of language and its conventions when writing, speaking, reading, or listening.
- Verify the preliminary determination of the meaning of a word or phrase (e.g., by checking the inferred meaning in context or in a dictionary).
- Acquire and use accurately grade-appropriate general academic and domain-specific words and phrases; gather vocabulary knowledge when considering a word or phrase important to comprehension or expression.

Teacher Tip!

I scour used bookstores and garage sales for pictures. Old coffee table books contain better photos for this activity. The activity is more effective when you do not use pictures of famous people or events. Use pictures of nature, locations, objects and everyday people.

Student Sample: Adjectives Abound

1. Pick your picture and paste it below.

2. When your three minutes begin, write as many adjectives as you can think of that describe your picture.

   yummy, small, sweet, neat, tasty, good, fancy, soft

   From the thesaurus: scrumptious, delectable, frosted, triangular, mountainous

3. Add to your list using the thesaurus.

4. Using your adjectives, write a paragraph about the picture in the space below.

   The owner of Scrumptious Bakery liked to make tasty frosted cupcakes. The mountainous, triangular piles of soft frosting made them extra good. They looked so neat and fancy that people bought lots of the small, sweet treats.

Figure 2.1

Adjectives Abound

Name:

Date:

1. Pick your picture and paste it below.

2. When your three minutes begin, write as many adjectives as you can think of that describe your picture.

3. Add to your list using the thesaurus.

4. Using your adjectives, write a paragraph about the picture in the space below.

_____

_____

_____

_____

_____

_____

Figure 2.2

Lesson Three

Adjectives Carousel

Overview and Tips for Classroom Implementation

Prompting the student writer to go beyond the most commonly used adjectives, the adjective carousel activity generates lists of adjectives that the student writer can use as a reference at a later date.

Lesson Instructions

First, begin by putting students in groups of three or four. Give each group the Adjectives Carousel handout (Figure 3.2), or a larger sheet of paper if desired. Each group's sheet has a different adjective written on it. One student in each group can be the recorder and is given a specific color marker. (Each group recorder has a different color marker so that at the end of the activity, you will know which group recorded the information on each chart paper.)

Next, instruct the students that they will be given thirty seconds to write down on their chart paper all of the synonyms that they can think of for the adjective listed on the chart paper. Also explain to the students that when time is called (displaying a timer can be helpful), they will pass their chart paper to the next group. The new group will add even more synonyms for the adjective listed on the chart paper. These exchanges will continue until every group has contributed synonyms to every adjective chart.

Skills Covered in this Lesson

- Verify the preliminary determination of the meaning of a word or phrase (e.g., by checking the inferred meaning in context or in a dictionary).
- Acquire and use accurately grade-appropriate general academic and domain-specific words and phrases; gather vocabulary knowledge when considering a word or phrase important to comprehension or expression.

Teacher Tips!

1. Start with common adjectives like colors or sizes – or use adjectives that are content related. It will be easier for the students to generate the lists. For older and more proficient students, choose adjectives that may be more geared toward college readiness.

2. After the second exchange, the groups will need additional time. On the third exchange, extend the time to 40 seconds, then 50 seconds and so on until all of the groups have contributed to each adjective chart. I also suggest that on the last rotation you give the students about 2-3 minutes so that they can add synonyms they find through an outside source, like a thesaurus. Post the completed adjective charts in the classroom or have students record the word lists and keep them in their writing folders.

Student Sample: Adjectives Carousel

Adjective: Stinky

1. Group 1 Synonyms:
   smelly, gross, disgusting

2. Group 2 Synonyms:
   aromatic, fragrant, rank

3. Group 3 Synonyms:
   offensive, repulsive

4. Group 4 Synonyms:
   noxious, putrid, revolting, icky

Figure 3.1

Adjectives Carousel

Name:

Date:

Adjective:

1. Group 1 Synonyms:

2. Group 2 Synonyms:

3. Group 3 Synonyms:

4. Group 4 Synonyms:

Figure 3.2

Lesson Four

Apostrophes in Public

Overview and Tips for Classroom Implementation

Authenticity is an essential element of effective language learning at any age – that means that examples should relate to lived experiences rather than just appear in books. This is one of my favorite strategies because it's authentic and students really enjoy it. In this activity students identify and correct "real world" examples of incorrect apostrophe usage. They are usually astounded at the number of errors they find on signs, in other printed material, and online. As you can imagine, adolescents are especially enthused to find grammar and punctuation errors on signs in their own community.

Lesson Instructions

First, distribute a variety of pictures and printed media examples to the students. Put the students in groups of two to four.

Next, use the Apostrophes in Public graphic organizer (Figure 4.2) for this assignment. Students should examine the pictures or printed media examples, identify the error, and explain why it is incorrect.

Skills Covered in this Lesson

- Demonstrate command of the conventions of standard English grammar and usage when writing or speaking.
- Demonstrate command of the conventions of standard English capitalization, punctuation, and spelling when writing.

Teacher Tips!

1. The Apostrophes in Public graphic organizer can be used as a formative assessment to determine if the students are internalizing the formation of contractions.

2. This activity is not limited to apostrophe errors; you can encourage students to look for other errors like spelling mistakes and misused "confusing" words (who's/whose, your/you're, to/two/too, etc.).
Take photos of mistakes you find in your own neighborhood or use examples you find online. There are many sources. Start by looking here:

apostropheabuse.com/

oxbridgeediting.co.uk/blog/funny-grammar-mistakes-apostrophes/

sharoncolon.com/sharon/pictures.htm

Student Sample: Apostrophes in Public

Directions: Using the distributed pictures, complete the following information in this graphic organizer.

Picture It! Copy the sentence, statement, or signage error.	Explain It! Explain why this is an error.	Fix it! Write the sentence, statement, or signage correctly.
Thank You Veteran's!	There shouldn't be an apostrophe in Veterans because the Veterans aren't possessing something.	Thank You Veterans!
The Ladies and Gentlemens Cloakrooms	Ladies and Gentlemens should have possessive apostrophes because of the cloakroom.	The Ladies' and Gentlemen's Cloakrooms

Figure 4.1

Apostrophes in Public

Name:

Date:

Directions: Using the distributed pictures, complete the following information in this graphic organizer.

Picture It! Copy the sentence, statement, or signage error.	Explain It! Explain why this is an error.	Fix it! Write the sentence, statement, or signage correctly.

Figure 4.2

Close the Literacy Achievement Gap: Doing Whatever it Takes

We deliver professional development for teachers using a combination of in-person presentations and workshops, live webinars, on-demand courses, and virtual office hours.

Engaging Learners has years of experience empowering educators with budget-friendly, research-based, and easy-to-administer solutions.

Contact us at
info@EngagingLearners.com
or call **(312) 576-8222**

to schedule a free, no-obligation phone consultation with Dr. McKnight

Lesson Five

Applicable Appositive

Overview and Tips for Classroom Implementation

An appositive is a noun or noun phrase that is placed beside another noun or a pronoun to explain or identify it. This activity can be used as an introduction to appositives or for review.

Lesson Instructions

First, group the students into pairs. Give each student 60 seconds to tell their partner a few facts about themselves.

Next, instruct the students to make a list of five things that they learned about their partner.

Then, instruct the students to write sentences about their partner that include appositive phrases. You can use the following examples for the students. Note that the appositive phrases in the examples are in italics.

> Katie, *the English teacher*, tries to make grammar lessons engaging.
>
> Snoopy, *a famous dog*, is a lovable cartoon character.
>
> Mrs. Blackwell, *the new principal at Southside High School*, is a big baseball fan.

Finally, invite the students to read their sentences with appositive phrases out loud and introduce their partners to the class.

Skills Covered in this Lesson

- Demonstrate command of the conventions of standard English grammar and usage when writing or speaking.

Teacher Tip!

This lesson is particularly useful at the beginning of the school year, when the students are getting to know each other. It is also helpful for the teacher to model sentences with appositive phrases for the students.

Student Sample: Applicable Appositive

My Name: Jeni Rosenberg
Partner's Name: Susan Kraynak

Five things I learned about my partner:

Susan takes dance classes and she likes to bake cookies and cupcakes. She has a dog named Muffy, a sister named Sarah and a brother named Steven. Her favorite class at school is art and her least favorite class is gym. Her best friend's name is Krissey.

Five sentences with appositive phrases about my partner:

1. Susan, a dancer, takes tap class.
2. Susan, the baker, makes snickerdoodle.
3. Susan, the dog lover, walks Muffy outside.
4. Susan, the artist, likes painting.
5. Susan, Krissey's friend, has one brother and one sister.

Figure 5.1

Applicable Appositive

My Name:

Partner's Name:

Date:

Five things I learned about my partner:

Five sentences with appositive phrases about my partner:

1. _____
2. _____
3. _____
4. _____
5. _____

Figure 5.2

Lesson Six

The Colon

Overview and Tips for Classroom Implementation

In this mini lesson, students will learn how to effectively use colons in writing. The colon is a useful punctuation mark for more complicated writing and to cue the audience when additional information is about to be introduced.

Lesson Instructions

First, prepare for the activity by writing the following phrases on heavy paper or card stock. Each set of phrase cards can be combined with a colon to form a complete sentence. Note that the colons are missing (for now). You'll need one set of phrase cards for each student.

Did you go // to the store // at 5 // 00 p.m.?

The following students // were finalists in // the spelling bee // Tayesha, Will, and Sophie.

My friend's // favorite movie // is Pirates of the Caribbean // Dead Men Tell No Tales.

Our whole class // agrees on one thing // we want to learn more // about zombie fungus.

In addition to the above phrase cards, make four cards with a colon punctuation mark. It's especially helpful to make the punctuation cards a different color than the sentence cards.

Next, begin by introducing or reviewing the proper use of colons. There are many online resources that explain the rules including one of my favorites, *Quick and Dirty Tips* by Mignon Fogary (a.k.a. "Grammar Girl").

quickanddirtytips.com/education/grammar/colons

You may prefer to use the following simplified set of rules.

The colon has three grammatical uses and a few non-grammatical uses:

Grammatical Uses

1. To introduce a list of items
   Example: All dogs need five things: food, water, shelter, exercise, and socialization.

2. Between independent clauses when the second explains or illustrates the first
   Example: I have very little time to learn about linear equations: the test is on Friday.

3. To emphasize a phrase or single word at the end of a sentence
   Example: The jury finally reached a verdict: not guilty.

Non-Grammatical Uses

1. To separate hours from minutes when writing time
   Example: School starts at 8:00 a.m.

2. After the salutation in a business letter
   Example: Dear Professor McKnight:

3. Between the title and subtitle of a book, article, or movie
   Example: *Frankenstein*: *The Modern Prometheus*

Then, divide the class into groups of four. Each group will be given a set of phrase cards and four colon punctuation cards.

Finally, instruct the students to work together to arrange the phrase cards and apply the punctuation card in order to form four complete sentences. After the students have completed the their sentences, have them present their work to their classmates. Encourage them to discuss their procedure and reasoning.

Figure 6.1

Skills Covered in this Lesson

- Demonstrate command of the conventions of standard English grammar and usage when writing or speaking.

Teacher Tips!

1. The complete sentences with correct colon usage are:
    Did you go to the store at 5:00 p.m.?
    The following students were finalists in the spelling bee: Tayesha, Will, and Sophie.
    My friend's favorite movie is *Pirates of the Caribbean: Dead Men Tell No Tales*.
    Our whole class agrees on one thing: we want to learn more about zombie fungus.

2. It is useful to post the colon rules at the front of the room so that the students have an easily accessible reference.

3. To adjust the rigor for struggling students, consider using different colors for each group of phrase cards. Using different colors helps students focus on four cards at a time and arrange those cards into a cogent sentence.

4. Students who have already mastered this skill, or who master it quickly, can be invited to take it a step further by writing their own sentences and creating phrase cards for their classmates to assemble. (Be sure to check their sentences for correct punctuation use before handing their work off to classmates!)

Lesson Seven

Commas, an Overview

Overview and Tips for Classroom Implementation

Commas are tough to teach and tough to master. Even English teachers can occasionally misuse a comma. This lesson provides an overview of the basic rules for commas. I suggest that this lesson be used as an introduction or a quick review, since it is comprehensive.

Lesson Instructions

First, prepare for this activity by referring to the Ten Quick Comma Rules in Figure 7.1. Gather ten separate poster boards or large sheets of construction paper and write one Quick Comma Rule, and its example sentence, on each one.

Next, divide the students into ten groups. Give each group a poster board with a different comma rule.

Then, provide the following directions:

1. Read your assigned comma rule and its example.
2. As a group, write one example sentence that demonstrates your understanding of that comma rule. This is a timed activity. You will have two minutes to write your example on the poster board. (Displaying a timer for the students can assist them to stay on task.)
3. When time is called, you will pass your poster board to the next group. Your group will receive a new poster board with another comma rule.

4. You will have two minutes to write one example sentence on the new poster board.
5. The process will repeat until every group has written at least one example for each of the ten comma rules.
6. Work together as a team! Use quiet voices to discuss your sentences and take turns writing.

Finally, after the students have written examples for each of the ten comma rules, the groups should look at the poster board with the rule that they were originally assigned. Instruct them to check each of the examples for accuracy.

Skills Covered in this Lesson

- Demonstrate command of the conventions of standard English grammar and usage when writing or speaking.

Teacher Tips!

1. Give each group a different color pen or marker so it will be easier for you to keep track of which examples belong to which student group.
2. You can adjust the rigor by increasing or decreasing the amount of time. The two-minute time limit won't work for every class.
3. Consider concluding the activity by handing out copies of the Ten Quick Comma Rules. Encourage students to keep them in their class notebooks for reference.

Ten Quick Comma Rules

(There are more comma rules but here are ten important ones for writers.)

1. Use commas to separate items in a list or series (words, phrases, and clauses).

Example: Colin enjoys trains, cars, and Dr. Seuss.

2. Use a comma after the words "yes" or "no" when these are used to start a sentence.

Example: Yes, I would like some dessert.

3. Use a comma to set off consecutive prepositional phrases when they begin a sentence.

Example: At the end of the day in Chicago, people rush home from work.

4. Use a comma after an introductory participle or participial phrase.

Example: Inspired by the professor's comments, Ellie decided to go to law school.

5. Use a comma after an introductory adverb clause.

Example: Before we boarded the airplane, we needed to pass through security.

6. Use a comma to separate two or more adjectives that are placed before a noun.

Example: My Girl Scout troop is a dedicated, kind group.

7. Use a comma to separate independent clauses joined by the conjunctions for, and, nor, but, or and yet.

Example: Troop 320 wanted to go camping, but it was too cold to sleep in tents.

8. Use a comma to cue a word or words in direct address.

Example: Jim, can you reach the top shelf?

9. Use a comma to cue a parenthetical expression like such as, I believe, and for example.

Example: This, I believe, is the best way to solve the problem.

10. Use a comma at the beginning and end of an appositive phrase.

Example: Susan, my dear friend, likes to kayak.

Figure 7.1

Lesson Eight

Commas, Part Two

Overview and Tips for Classroom Implementation

There are many rules for commas. This is one of the reasons why it is easy to make errors in comma usage. These five comma rules are the easier ones to master and remember.

Lesson Instructions

First, make copies of Five More Comma Rules (see Figure 8.2) for each student. The students can place a copy, for reference, in their writing folder or classroom notebook.

Next, prior to the lesson, create Comma Rules envelopes for each pair of students with the following contents:

- A complete set of the sentence strips (see Figure 8.1)
- Ten Commas (see Figure 8.1)
- Directions for the activity (see Figure 8.1)

Finally, assign an envelope to a pair of students. Each student pair will "dump" the contents from the envelope and insert commas where needed for each sentence.

Skills Covered in this Lesson

- Demonstrate command of the conventions of standard English grammar and usage when writing or speaking.

Teacher Tips!

1. Use a timer. In most cases, five minutes will be plenty of time for the student pairs to complete the activity.
2. Print the commas on different colored paper. This helps students visually sort and categorize the information.

Ten Commas

Directions: In this envelope there are ten sentences that need commas. Using your "Five More Comma Rules" reference sheet, use the comma cards to place them where they are needed.

,	,	,	,
,	,	,	,
,	,	,	,

- Dear Aunt Loretta Thanks for the birthday card.
- Her birthday is on July 15 1998.
- Tanisha can you open the window some more?
- The band performed in Chicago New York London and Paris.
- Our friends who are always thoughtful made us some cookies for the party.
- More determined than ever the baseball player swung even harder.
- Mr. King the well known author has another best seller.
- The long exhausting swim lesson finally finished.
- "I moved from London to New York" the model explained.
- The editor asked "Are you sure that you can meet the deadline?"

Figure 8.1

Five More Comma Rules

1. Use a comma after the salutation in a letter or email.

Example: Dear Mom,

2. Use a comma after the closing in a letter or email.

Example: Sincerely,

3. Use a comma to separate items in dates and addresses:

Examples:

July 9, 2001

1600 Pennsylvania Ave., Washington, D.C.

4. Use a comma to separate the speaker from the speaker's direct quotation.

Example: "I need to ask you a question," Ellie said.

5. Use a comma after a mild interjection.

Example: Oh, you startled me.

Figure 8.2

Lesson Nine

Comma Match

Overview and Tips for Classroom Implementation

This lesson provides continued practice and application of the comma rules. The students will work in teams to match the rules with the different examples.

Lesson Instructions

First, divide the class into groups of three to four students. Each student will need an envelope with the following:

> Cards with each comma rule (see Figure 9.1). Print these cards on light blue paper or card stock.
>
> Cards with the examples (see Figure 9.2). Print these cards on yellow paper or card stock.

You will need to make the envelopes for this activity before you conduct this lesson.

Next, once the students have been divided into groups with three to four members, provide the following directions:

> *Match the reasons or rules for using a comma (these cards are light blue) with the examples. The examples are printed on yellow cards. You have five minutes to complete this activity.*

In addition to providing these instructions verbally, be sure to write them down on the chalkboard or on the envelopes that the students are using for this activity.

Then, as the students are working, be sure to circulate among the groups. This is a great opportunity to clarify instructions and answer questions.

Skills Covered in this Lesson

- Demonstrate command of the conventions of standard English grammar and usage when writing or speaking.

Teacher Tip!

Be sure to print the comma rules on colored paper and the examples on a different colored paper. This helps the students to organize the information. In addition, it makes it easier for you to observe the students as they work on this activity.

Comma Rules

- Use a comma after the salutation in a letter or email.
- Use a comma to separate items in dates and addresses.
- Use a comma to set off consecutive prepositional phrases when they begin a sentence.
- Use a comma to separate two or more adjectives that are placed before a noun.
- Use a comma to set off a word or words in a direct address.

Figure 9.1

Comma Rules Examples

- Dear Jim, Thanks for the birthday card.
- I was married on August 10, 1991.
- At the beginning of the day, the rooster crowed.
- An informed, trained representative will help you.
- Juanita, don't forget to finish your homework!

Figure 9.2

Lesson Ten

Common Nouns

Overview and Tips for Classroom Implementation

Nouns are one of the eight parts of speech. This activity introduces the characteristics of the common noun and provides an opportunity for students to practice identifying both singular and plural common nouns.

Lesson Instructions

First, you will need two large sheets of butcher paper. Label one sheet "Singular Common Nouns" and the other "Plural Common Nouns." You will also need a marker for each student in the class. Put one sheet of paper in the front of the classroom and the other sheet in the back of the classroom.

Next, review the following information with the students:

> **Nouns** name a person, place, thing or idea.
>
> **Common Nouns** begin with a small (or lowercase) letter and can be either singular or plural. Common nouns are also nonspecific.

Singular Common Nouns name one person, place, thing or idea.
Example: student (person), classroom (place), pencil (thing), education (idea)

Plural Common Nouns name more than one person, place, thing or idea.
Example: students (more than one person), classrooms (more than one place), pencils (more than one thing), educations (more than one idea)
Notice that you usually add "s" or "es" to make a common noun plural.

Then, divide the students into two groups. One group will be assigned to the "Singular Common Nouns" and one group will be assigned to the "Plural Common Nouns."

Next, instruct the students to look around the classroom and identify as many common nouns as they can. When you say "go," the students are to write down, as fast as they can, any common nouns. Students in the "Singular Common Noun" group write down only singular common nouns, students in the "Plural Common Noun" group write down only plural common nouns. Give the students about two minutes. Once time is called, have the groups switch positions. Repeat the activity.

Finally, review the submissions as part of a whole class or large group activity. Discuss the words that students wrote down and make corrections as necessary. Encourage students to explain their reasoning.

Skills Covered in this Lesson

- Use knowledge of language and its conventions when writing, speaking, reading, or listening.

Teacher Tips!

1. Once the students have completed both posters, give them a few minutes to read the words their classmates have written. That way they'll be prepared for the large group discussion.
2. I like to create a handout with the information about common nouns using their words as the examples. I encourage students to keep the handout in their writing folders for reference.

Notes

Lesson Eleven

Connecting Clauses

Overview and Tips for Classroom Implementation

This lesson gives students the opportunity to practice using punctuation when combining clauses. This is a tricky writing skill for students. The students will review the basic rules for independent clauses and dependent clauses. Next, they will connect clauses using what they have learned.

Lesson Instructions

First, prior to conducting the lesson, you will need the following:

Handouts for dependent and independent clauses (see Figure 11.2). You will need one copy for each student. They can put these in their writing folders for future reference.

Cut 4 x 6 index cards into two pieces making sure that each side has a unique shape that connects only with the other card. In other words, you are making two connecting puzzle pieces out of each index card.

Next, when the students enter the class, hand each of them a puzzle piece. The students will find the classmate that matches their puzzle piece. Once the students have found their puzzle match, they are to sit together as partners for the mini lesson.

Then, distribute the "Clause Rules" handout (see Figure 11.2). Using the examples on the "Clause Rules" handout, the students are to write sentences that join clauses with appropriate punctuation on the index cards. They can flip the cards over so they'll have two index card puzzles. They can write two sentences. The final product will look like this:

Figure 11.1

Skills Covered in this Lesson

- Demonstrate command of the conventions of standard English grammar and usage when writing or speaking.

- Demonstrate command of the conventions of standard English capitalization, punctuation, and spelling when writing.

Teacher Tips!

1. I always collect the students' puzzle pieces and check for accuracy. The puzzle pieces can also be used for review in class the next day. Distribute them and encourage the students to review and practice the "Clause Rules".

2. Feel free to adapt this lesson as necessary. Sometimes I concentrate on dependent clauses and independent clauses separately. I also have treated dependent marker words, independent marker words, and FANBOYS conjunctions as separate lessons.

Clause Rules

An **Independent Clause** is a group of words that contains a subject and verb, and it expresses a complete thought. An independent clause can be written as a sentence.

Examples: *The dog grew tired.*
He ran around the house.

A **Dependent Clause** is a group of words that contains a subject and verb, but does not express a complete thought. A dependent clause is not a sentence.

Examples: *when the dog ran around the house*
before he grew tired

How to Connect Clauses

Dependent Marker Word – A dependent marker word is a word added to the beginning of an *independent* clause which turns it into a *dependent* clause.

Examples: *The dog grew tired **when** he ran around the house.*
***When** the dog ran around the house, he grew tired.*

Punctuation tip: If the second clause in a sentence is *dependent*, you don't need a comma. If the second clause in a sentence is *independent*, you need a comma.

Common dependent marker words: *after, although, as if, because, before, even if, even though, if, in order to, since, though, unless, until, whatever, when, whenever, whether, while*

Coordinating Conjunctions (FANBOYS) – The seven coordinating conjunctions used as connecting words at the beginning of a clause are **F**or, **A**nd, **N**or, **B**ut, **O**r, **Y**et, **S**o.

Examples: *The dog ran around the house **and** grew tired.*
*The dog grew tired, **yet** he ran around the house.*

Punctuation tip: If the second clause in a sentence is *dependent*, you don't need a comma. If the second clause in a sentence is *independent*, you need a comma.

Independent Marker Word – An independent marker word is a connecting word used at the beginning of an *independent* clause. It doesn't change the independent clause into a dependent clause. In other words, both clauses express complete thoughts.

Examples: *The dog ran around the house; **therefore**, he grew tired.*
*The dog grew tired; **nevertheless**, he ran around the house.*

Punctuation tip: When the second independent clause in a sentence begins with an independent marker word, you need to use a semicolon.

Common independent marker words: *also, consequently, furthermore, however, moreover, nevertheless, therefore*

Figure 11.2

Lesson Twelve

Dependent Clauses

Overview and Tips for Classroom Implementation

This advanced grammar activity reinforces understanding of independent and dependent clauses. Understanding this distinction supports student writing. The mini lesson focuses on indicators that will help students to identify the difference between the two types of clauses, and the follow-up activity gives student writers an opportunity to practice turning a dependent clause into a complete thought.

Lesson Instructions

First, prior to conducting the lesson in class, create activity envelopes that contain the materials found in Figure 12.1. Each envelope should contain a definition sheet and the dependent and independent clause strips.

Next, divide the class into groups that contain three students each. Give an activity envelope to each student group. Read the directions for the activity and instruct the students to begin. As the students work on the activity, circulate among them to make sure that they are on task and to troubleshoot any questions or difficulties that they might have with the task.

Then, call time after five minutes and go over the answers as a large group.

Materials for Lesson Twelve

Directions: Copy this page and cut out the Definitions for Independent and Dependent Clauses, the sentence strips, and activity directions. The definitions and sentence strips should be placed in an envelope. You will need one envelope for each group of three students.

Definitions for Independent and Dependent Clauses:

Independent Clause – a group of words that contains a subject and verb, and it expresses a complete thought. An independent clause can be written as a sentence.

Dependent Clause – a group of words that contains a subject and verb, but does not express a complete thought. A dependent clause is not a sentence. Often, a dependent clause is marked by a dependent marker word.

Dependent Marker Word – a word added to the beginning of an independent clause which turns it into a dependent clause.

Examples: *after, although, as, as if, because, before, even if, even though, if, in order to, since, though, unless, until, whatever, when, whenever, whether, while*

In addition to delivering directions orally, print the directions and paste it to the outside of each activity envelope.

Directions for Activity

When it is time to begin, read the definitions of dependent and independent clauses, as well as dependent marker words.

Examine the clause strips and determine whether each is an independent or dependent clause.

After you have sorted all the clause strips, revise the dependent clauses to turn them into independent clauses that convey complete thoughts or ideas.

Figure 12.1

- Because the team won the game last week
- As the actor exited the scene
- Since I haven't been to the doctor
- Colin acts like he has never seen a movie before
- Though I wanted to go to the exhibit
- Everyone had a good time
- Chocolate is delicious
- Until the review board makes a decision about the student
- In order to get a prize
- He drove to the store
- Whenever she goes to the grocery store
- Even if he gets a raise
- Even I can guess the answer
- Although we have a curfew
- Although the map revealed a secret passage
- I know that it is snowing outside
- Maybe if it snows

Figure 12.1

Lesson Thirteen

End Punctuation Marks

Overview and Tips for Classroom Implementation

This lesson is designed to review periods, question marks, and exclamation marks.

Lesson Instructions

First, prior to conducting the lesson in class, create activity envelopes that contain the materials found in Figure 13.1. Write or cut-and-paste the activity instructions to the front of each activity envelope. Cut the sentence strips apart, and cut each of the punctuation rules apart. Each envelope should contain a copy of: rules and examples for the use of a period, rules and examples for the use of a question mark, rules and examples for the use of an exclamation point, and a set of unpunctuated sentence strips. You will need an activity envelope for each student group.

Next, divide the class into groups that contain three to four students. Give each group one of the envelopes and instruct the students to follow the directions for the activity.

Then, as the students work in groups to complete the activity, circulate to answer any questions and to monitor progress. Once the students complete the activity, you can review the answers with them through a large group discussion.

Skills Covered in this Lesson

- Demonstrate command of the conventions of standard English capitalization, punctuation, and spelling when writing.
- Use context (e.g., the overall meaning of a sentence or paragraph; a word's position or function in a sentence) as a clue to the meaning of a word or phrase.

Teacher Tip!

Print each lesson component in a different color. It makes it easier for the students to sort and categorize the information.

Materials for Lesson Thirteen

Activity Directions

In this envelope is a set of rules for periods, question marks, and exclamation points. Examine each sentence and determine which end punctuation mark is needed. Using each of the rules as a header, place the sentences under the corresponding end-punctuation marks.

Period – Rules and Examples

Use a period at the end of a declarative sentence, a sentence that is a polite request, and a sentence that includes a mild command.

Examples: Stefan likes peanut butter. Please wait in the hall. Hand me that eraser.

Question Mark – Rules and Examples

Use a question mark at the end of an interrogative sentence.

Examples: How many students were in class today? Did you ever wear green shoes? Where will Brianna go on her vacation? Who said so?

Exclamation Point – Rules and Examples

Use an exclamation point to indicate strong feelings or a raised voice in speech.

Examples: I passed my driver's test! There's a spider on my seat! Look at those beautiful flowers! Careful!

Figure 13.1

Materials for Lesson Thirteen

Can you remember how many coins are in the collection

"I wish that I had something to give you," my sister said

Let's see what surprises are at the end of the story

Because the team won the game last week

Who has the answer to the request

Tell them all to hurry up

Should the vegetables go in the refrigerator

I like that photo of you

Where are the photocopies for the project

Cool You can see all of the colors in the rainbow

Figure 13.1

"Juicy at home learning for teachers."

*–Letitia Scott
Literacy Teacher*

Engaging Learners Academy

The **Engaging Learners Academy** is your source for **On-Demand Professional Development**, promoting **practical, effective strategies** for the **K-12 educator**. The Engaging Learners Academy provides research-based solutions that real classroom teachers want to use, and that real students actually respond to.

Topics include:
- Literacy & Learning Centers: Building Literacy Skills and Content Knowledge
- Advancing Differentiation: Thinking and Learning for the 21st Century
- Grading and Assessment for the Modern Classroom: Standards Based Grading and Formative Assessment
- Disciplinary Literacy for the Content Areas
- How to Foster Resilience in a Trauma-Sensitive Classroom: Strategies to Promote Social-Emotional Learning (SEL)

And more!

Visit us at **Engaging Learners Academy** online!

Ask about group discounts and "all access" passes.
info@engaginglearners.com
(312) 576-8222
Want to get training on your own?
Teachers are welcome to enroll independently!

Lesson Fourteen

Fragments and Run-Ons

Overview and Tips for Classroom Implementation

This lesson is designed to introduce sentence fragments and run-on sentences, two of the most complex concepts to teach young writers. Be prepared to teach multiple lessons on the topic and plan to give students plenty of opportunity to practice sentence fragment and run-on correction.

Lesson Instructions

First, prior to the lesson, write the following definitions on three large poster boards:

Sentence: A sentence expresses a complete thought. A sentence usually contains a subject and a verb, although sometimes it can be a single word (Go!).

Fragment: A fragment is a group of words that doesn't express a complete thought. A fragment often lacks a subject or a verb, unlike a complete sentence.

Run-On Sentence: A run-on sentence is two or more sentences that are incorrectly written as one sentence.

Post each poster board with the definition in a different area of the classroom. Cut out the sentences, fragments, and run-on sentences from Figure 14.1. Print and cut out multiple sets if necessary.

Next, review the definitions of sentence, fragment, and run on-sentence with students. Refer to the posters.

Then, divide the students into pairs. Give each pair two sentences, fragments or sentence run-ons from Figure 14.1. Instruct the students to read the definition poster boards and match their sentence, fragment or sentence run-on. You can give the students tape so that the strips of paper with the sentences, fragments, and run-ons can be attached to the correct corresponding definition poster board.

Finally, review the definitions and the students' posting of the sentences, fragments, and run-ons.

Skills Covered in this Lesson

- Demonstrate command of the conventions of standard English capitalization, punctuation, and spelling when writing.
- Use knowledge of language and its conventions when writing, speaking, reading or listening.

Teacher Tip!

The first time you introduce these concepts, you can color code the strips of paper (e.g., print sentences on green paper, sentence fragments on pink paper, and run-ons on yellow paper). Use the same colors for each corresponding definition poster board. As students tape the strips to the poster boards, encourage them to explain to their partners why it belongs on that poster board.

Materials for Lesson Fourteen

Directions: Cut out each of the sentences, fragments, and run-ons.

- Have you already eaten the ice cream?
- At the beginning of the story.
- Let's take the picture, we like the background for it.
- Entering the interstate at the end of the trip.
- Several clerks tried to help me finally I decided to leave.
- During the party at the end of the holiday season.
- I like to attend the baseball game.
- I ate ice cream at the carnival.
- Before they entered the contest.
- After all of the applause for the audience.
- I enjoyed the performance.
- I need to get more information for the research report.
- Please pass me the spices so I can finish making the pizza.
- There are so many choices I can't make a decision.
- The workers building the skyscraper are good they can finish the job in time.

Figure 14.1

Lesson Fifteen

Further vs. Farther

Overview and Tips for Classroom Implementation

Further and *farther* is often a confusing word pair for young writers. This activity provides students practice in determining when to use further and farther.

Lesson Instructions

First, review the following definitions for *further* and *farther* with the students.

Further is used to mean longer or more.

> **Examples:**
>
> This position can go no *further*.
>
> In Australia, the American dollar goes *further*.
>
> I want to study Spanish *further*.

Farther is used when discussing distance.

> **Examples:**
>
> I'm too tired to walk *farther*.
>
> Ellie lives *farther* from my house than I thought.

Next, distribute two index cards to each student. One card should be labeled "further" and the other card should be labeled "farther".

Then, display the practice sentences for the students (on an overhead projector, LCD projector, etc.). Show each sentence, one at a time, and ask the students to indicate if *further* or *farther* should be used by holding up the corresponding card.

Sample Sentences:

    The boy shot the slingshot (farther/further) than I did.

    The police officer waited for (farther/further) instructions.

    Can you throw the ball any (farther/further)?

    She lives (farther/further) from the school than I do.

    The parents waited for (farther/further) information about the college.

    Without (farther/further) discussion, Leo and Chris entered the haunted house.

Skills Covered in this Lesson

- Use knowledge of language and its conventions when writing, speaking, reading, or listening.

Teacher Tip!

Once the students have responded to the sample sentences, they can create their own sentences that use *further* and *farther*.

Notes

Lesson Sixteen

Homonyms

Overview and Tips for Classroom Implementation

Homonyms are sound-alike words that are easily confused. They are particularly troublesome for English language learners, and that is why it is important for us to explicitly teach homonyms.

Lesson Instructions

First, in preparation for the lesson, print a copy of the "Common Homonyms" handout (see Figure 16.1). You'll need one for each student. Also write each common homonym on a separate index card.

Next, distribute a copy of the handout and one card to each student.

Then, divide the class into groups of four to five students. Instruct the students that they need to create a tableau (see Figure 16.2 & 16.3) for each homonym from the index cards.

Finally, as the students present each homonym tableau, the class guesses which homonym is being represented.

Skills Covered in this Lesson

- Demonstrate command of the conventions of standard English capitalization, punctuation, and spelling when writing.
- Use knowledge of language and its conventions when writing, speaking, reading, or listening.

Teacher Tips!

1. In order to speed up the pacing for the homonym tableaux, I always ask the groups to present each one in quick succession.
2. Ask students to plan their tableaux on paper and illustrate how they're going to "act out" the homonyms.
3. At the end of the activity, students should keep their copy of the "Common Homonyms" handout in their writing folder to use as a reference.

Common Homonyms

board/bored	break/brake	capital/capitol	choose/chews
desert/dessert	formally/formerly	hear/here	its/it's
loose/lose	quiet/quite	peace/piece	plain/plane
principal/principle	scene/seen	sweet/suite	there/their/they're
theirs/there's	throw/throe	threw/through	to/too/two
tow/toe	waist/waste	way/weigh	weak/week
wear/where	weather/whether	who's/whose	whirled/world
when/wend	witch/which	would/wood	your/you're

Figure 16.1

Student Sample: Homonym Tableaux

Group Members: Jessie, Diego, Tom, Brenda

Date: 10/13/2019

scene / seen

break / brake

sweet / suite

weak / week

Figure 16.2

Homonym Tableaux Planning Sheet

Group Members:

Date:

- - - - - - - - -   - - - - - - - - -

- - - - - - - - -   - - - - - - - - -

Figure 16.3

Lesson Seventeen

Hyphens

Overview and Tips for Classroom Implementation

Hyphens are helpful punctuation marks that writers use to indicate to the reader when there are more syllables or connected words. Word processing has virtually eliminated the need to use hyphens to divide polysyllabic words at the end of a line by keeping words intact and automatically adjust spacing. However, we use the hyphen in English for words like, father-in-law. English also uses hyphens between two words that comprise a single adjective such as good-natured.

Lesson Instructions

First, review with students the following rules for hyphens.

Use a hyphen:

- to syllabicate words at the end of a line when typing or writing.
- to separate portions of certain compound words like merry-go-round, check-up, or brother-in-law.
- between two words that comprise a single adjective like mean-spirited, 4-page document, or happy-go-lucky.

Next, divide the group into pairs. Give each pair of students a poster board or large sheet of construction paper. Instruct the students to create a poster that illustrates each of the three conditions for using a hyphen. Their posters should state the hyphen rule and provide an example with an illustration.

Skills Covered in this Lesson

- Use knowledge of language and its conventions when writing, speaking, reading or listening.

Teacher Tip!

It is important for students to create visuals that correspond with the different conditions for using hyphens in writing. The pairing of a strong visual with the hyphen rule supports students' understanding of the punctuation concept.

Student Sample: Homonym Poster

Name: Ashley Brunson

Use a hyphen to separate portions of certain compound words.

A **MERRY** child **GO**ing a**ROUND** on a merry-go-round.

Figure 17.1

Lesson Eighteen

Idiomatic Expressions, Part One

Overview and Tips for Classroom Implementation

Idiomatic expressions are particularly problematic for English language learners because the meaning is implied, not directly stated. Most idiomatic expressions have cultural references that have been long forgotten, even by native English speakers.

Lesson Instructions

First, you will need to photocopy Figure 18.1 for student handouts. The phrases listed on the handout are a sample of the many idiomatic expressions that are commonly used in American English.

Next, distribute the handouts and ask the students to guess the meaning of each idiomatic expression. The students can work either independently or in pairs.

Then, using a variety of sources, have the students verify the guess. An idiomatic dictionary and various websites (listed below) will help the students to verify the guess. Using the websites and reference books, have the students trace the origin of some more common idiomatic expressions.

Helpful websites include:

idiomsite.com

usingenglish.com/reference/idioms

yourdictionary.com

Finally, ask the students to share their answers with the class and how they created a definition for each idiomatic expression. Tally the students to see how many of their guesses were accurate.

Skills Covered in this Lesson

- Demonstrate understanding of figurative language, word relationships, and nuances in word meanings.
- Acquire and use accurately grade-appropriate general academic and domain-specific words and phrases; gather vocabulary knowledge when considering a word or phrase important to comprehension or expression.

Teacher Tip!

In addition to their completing the handout, I always like to have the students illustrate the idiomatic expressions. Visualization is essential for vocabulary internalization.

© 2021 Engaging Learners, LLC

Idiomatic Expressions

Name:

Date:

Directions: Guess the meaning of each of the following idiomatic expressions. On the Internet, look for websites like idiomsite.com or usingenglish.com/reference/idioms to verify each of your guesses. You can also use these websites to discover the origin of these idiomatic expressions.

Idiomatic Expression	Guess the Meaning	Verify the Meaning	Origin of the Idiomatic Expression
a picture paints a thousand words			
back seat driver			
bad hair day			
break a leg			
chip on his shoulder			
cut to the chase			
diamond in the rough			
face the music			
Houston, we have a problem			
nerd			
like a chicken without its head			
OK			
pedal to the metal			
play by ear			
raining cats and dogs			

Figure 18.1

Lesson Nineteen

Idiomatic Expressions, Part Two

Overview and Tips for Classroom Implementation

Lesson 19 provides students with additional practice about idiomatic expressions. Learning about idiomatic expressions is particularly useful for English language learners since the meaning is implied and not directly stated. Most idiomatic expressions have cultural references that have been long forgotten, even by native English speakers.

Lesson Instructions

First, you will need to photocopy Figure 19.1 for student handouts. The phrases listed on the handout are a sample of the many idiomatic expressions that are commonly used in American English. Distribute the handouts and ask the students to guess the meaning of each idiomatic expression. The students can work either independently or in pairs.

Next, using a variety of sources, have the students verify the guess. An idiomatic dictionary and various websites (listed below) will help the students to verify the guess. Using the websites and reference books, have the students trace the origin of some of our more common idiomatic expressions.

Helpful websites include:

idiomsite.com

usingenglish.com/reference/idioms

yourdictionary.com

Then, ask the students to share their answers with the class and how they created a definition for each idiomatic expression. Tally the students to see how many of their guesses were accurate.

Skills Covered in this Lesson

- Demonstrate understanding of figurative language, word relationships, and nuances in word meanings.
- Acquire and use accurately grade-appropriate general academic and domain-specific words and phrases; gather vocabulary knowledge when considering a word or phrase important to comprehension or expression.

Teacher Tip!

In addition to their completing the handout, I always like to have the students illustrate the idiomatic expressions. Visualization is essential for vocabulary internalization.

Idiomatic Expressions: Part Two

Name:

Date:

Directions: Guess the meaning of each of the following idiomatic expressions. On the Internet, look for websites like idiomsite.com or usingenglish.com/reference/idioms to verify each of your guesses. You can also use these websites to discover the origin of these idiomatic expressions.

Idiomatic Expression	Guess the Meaning	Verify the Meaning	Origin of the Idiomatic Expression
apple of my eye			
back to square one			
none of your beeswax			
brownie points			
close, but no cigar			
deadline			
Elvis has left the building			
wake up on the wrong side of the bed			
knock on wood			
Murphy's Law			
Peeping Tom			
shot in the dark			
tongue in cheek			
under the weather			

Figure 19.1

Lesson Twenty

Its and It's

Overview and Tips for Classroom Implementation

I think there are many teachers who would agree that "its" and "it's" are often confused by students. As a writing teacher, I have taught the difference between its and it's multiple times. Here is a mini lesson to remind our students the difference between this commonly confused word pair.

Lesson Instructions

First, review with students the difference between "its" and "it's".

Its is the possessive form of *it*.
It's is a contraction combining the words *it* and *is*.

Next, distribute two index cards to each student and instruct them to write "its" on one card and "it's" on a second card. Pass out the Its and It's Worksheet.

Project the example sentences in Figure 20.1 for the students. As you display and read each sentence, have the students hold up the index card that provides the correct answer, either "its" or "it's", and have the students circle the correct answer on the It's and Its Worksheet.

Skills Covered in this Lesson

- Demonstrate command of the conventions of standard English capitalization, punctuation, and spelling when writing.

Teacher Tip!

I like to have the two index cards color-coded so when I am checking the students' responses, it is faster for me to determine if the correct answer is being displayed.

Its and It's Worksheet

Name:

Date:

1. _____ (Its, It's) getting cold outside.

2. I am learning how to play chess. _____ (Its, It's) a challenging game.

3. Let's portray _____ (its, it's) message more clearly.

4. I am thinking _____ (its, it's) owner should be contacted.

5. We know _____ (its, it's) hard to get the correct answer.

6. _____ (Its, It's) going to be easier to sell the house.

7. The team needs to work together in order to reach _____ (its, it's) full potential.

8. I like to bake cookies because _____ (its, it's) relaxing for me.

9. _____ (Its, It's) value is hard to determine in this volatile financial market.

Figure 20.1

Lesson Twenty-One
Metaphorical Expressions

Overview and Tips for Classroom Implementation

The use of metaphors in writing can help authors to create pictures and images for the reader. Many words have both literal and figurative meanings. Literal meanings might be more common, but metaphorical expressions can be powerful tools for expression. They can help us explain and understand our world in a non-literal way.

Lesson Instructions

First, explain metaphor to the students:

> A metaphor is an association of two objects by saying that one of them is the other.
>
> A metaphor compares two objects, but does not use the words *like*, *as*, or *than*.
>
> A metaphor creates strong images and pictures for the audience.

Next, discuss the following examples of metaphor:

> My sister is a bear in the morning.
>
> The stars are the flashlights of the night sky.
>
> She has the heart of an angel.

Then, divide the students into pairs and give each pair a Metaphorical Expressions handout (see Figure 21.2). Instruct the students to choose a famous person. The students should make a list of things (that aren't other people) to which a famous person could be compared. Have the students create a list of metaphorical expressions for the famous person.

Skills Covered in this Lesson

- Demonstrate understanding of figurative language, word relationships, and nuances in word meanings.

Teacher Tip!

You can have the students read the metaphors in class and have the others guess and identify the famous person.

Student Sample: Metaphorical Expressions

Celebrity: Lady Gaga

List of comparisons: A yellow finch, a musical instrument, an alien, a queen, a politician, Halloween. Lady Gaga has the singing voice of a yellow finch.

Metaphorical Expressions: She is a musical instrument.
Lady Gaga is the alien of the celebrity world.
Lady Gaga is the Queen of the pop music Kingdom.
Lady Gaga has the heart of a Halloween party.

Figure 21.1

Metaphorical Expressions

Group Members:

Date:

Celebrity: _____

List of Comparisons: _____
_____
_____
_____
_____
_____

Metaphorical Expressions: _____
_____
_____
_____
_____
_____
_____
_____
_____

Figure 21.2

Lesson Twenty-Two

Modifiers are Dangling

Overview and Tips for Classroom Implementation

Modifiers are words or phrases that clarify, or give more detail about, an idea or concept. A modifier is considered dangling when it isn't clear what is being modified because the intended subject is missing from the sentence.

Lesson Instructions

First, explain the following example to the students:

Having prepared dinner, the radio was turned on.

"Having prepared" states an action but it doesn't name the doer of this action. The doer must be the subject of the main clause that follows.

Next, discuss with the students the following strategies for correcting dangling modifiers:

- Name the doer of the action in the main clause.
- Change the phrase that dangles into a complete introductory clause by naming the doer of the action in that clause.

Then, divide the students into pairs. Copy the sample sentences with dangling modifiers and distribute to the student pairs (see Figure 22.1). Have the students correct the examples.

Practicing Correcting Sentences with Dangling Modifiers

Name:

Date:

Directions: Correct the sentences on your own. Then check your work with the revised sentences.

1. After reading the book, the ending was unsatisfying.

   Revision: _____

2. Leaving for the next train, your trip should be fine.

   Revision: _____

3. The experiment was a success, not having followed correct procedures.

   Revision: _____

4. After getting the job, the work was not satisfying.

   Revision: _____

5. Once I left for the office, it started to rain.

   Revision: _____

6. Knowing what the outcome might be, the movie was not enjoyable.

   Revision: _____

Figure 22.1

Skills Covered in this Lesson

- Use knowledge of language and its conventions when writing, speaking, reading or listening.

Teacher Tip!

As an extension activity, ask the students to create sentences with dangling modifiers that need to be corrected.

Suggested Revisions: Student answers may look something like this.

1. After reading the book, I thought that the ending was unsatisfying.
2. Leaving for the next train, you should be able to have a fine trip.
3. Their experiment was a success, not having followed correct procedures.
4. After getting the job, I thought that the work was not satisfying.
5. Once I left for the office, I noticed that it started to rain.
6. Knowing what the outcome might be, I thought that the movie was not enjoyable.

Figure 22.2

Lesson Twenty-Three

Onomatopoeia

Overview and Tips for Classroom Implementation

Onomatopoeia is a figure of speech which imitates the word that it represents. Words like "bang," "pop," and "click" are onomatopoeias that many students use in their everyday speech. Comic books and graphic novels often pair onomatopoeias with illustrations to great effect. Poets use onomatopoeic words because they are descriptive, specific, and help the reader imagine the scene. Writers like Edgar Allen Poe are well known for their masterful use of onomatopoeia in poems like "The Bells."

Lesson Instructions

Begin by having students watch the following videos which introduce and explain onomatopoeia:

onomatopoeia
youtube.com/watch?v=q-BVwwKTjll

Mrs. Munger's Class - Season 2 - Onomatopoeia
youtube.com/watch?v=evUzS6K-5Wg&feature=related

Prior to this lesson, collect a variety of inexpensive windup toys like those that come with kids' meals.

First, divide the students into pairs and ask each pair of students to select a toy.

Next, give the students two minutes to brainstorm words that they could use to describe the toy's sounds.

Then, when the students have a list of descriptive words, ask them to sort out those words that are onomatopoeia. (Tip: encourage students to say the descriptive words aloud to determine if they sound like what they represent. If not, those words are not onomatopoeia. They are likely to include words like quiet, funny, loud, and cute. These words are not onomatopoeias.)

Finally, invite student pairs to write a complete sentence about the toy that contains onomatopoeia.

Skills Covered in this Lesson

- Use knowledge of language and its conventions when writing, speaking, reading or listening.

Teacher Tip!

Using onomatopoeia, the students can create a brief four to six-line poem about their toy.

Hands-On Support for Teachers

means measurable literacy growth for students

Contact us at
info@EngagingLearners.com
or call **(312) 576-8222**

to schedule a free, no-obligation phone consultation with Dr. McKnight

Professional Development with Engaging Learners

We work with school leadership to create customized professional development to address each school's unique challenges. Whether you're looking for a 1-day presentation, training webinars, a hands-on workshop, or ongoing support, our PD leaders will help your teachers achieve amazing literacy growth.

Visit **www.EngagingLearners.com/on-site** for more info.

Lesson Twenty-Four

Placing Prepositions

Overview and Tips for Classroom Implementation

Prepositions serve as "locators" in space and time. When students understand how to identify and use prepositions in writing, they become more skilled in adding spatial and temporal detail.

Lesson Instructions

In this lesson we will focus on prepositions that describe how two things relate to each other in space. You will need a small toy car and a small cutout of a person for each student pair. Begin by explaining prepositions by demonstrating the relationship between the cutout person and the toy car. For example, the person can be "on top of the car" or "in the car."

First, divide the students into pairs. Give each student pair a car and person cutout.

Next, instruct the students to write as many statements, in the present tense, about the cutout person and the car. Give the students about five minutes to create and state as many relationships as possible between the cutout person and the toy car.

Then, give the students the list of common prepositions (see Figure 24.1). Instruct the students to review the list and to identify how many prepositions they used.

Finally, in a large class discussion, discuss what prepositions do in language and for our writing. Be sure to discuss the following:

Prepositions signal and introduce the answer to the question *Where?* They can also be used to answer the question *When?*

What prepositions can we use to describe how events relate to each other in time? Consider inviting students to use a preposition to describe how two of their written statements relate to each other in time.

For example:

- The person went toward the car and then went in the car.
  (These words all serve as prepositions: *toward*, *then*, and *in*.)
- The person was underneath the car until he went above the car.
  (These words all serve as prepositions: *underneath*, *until*, and *above*.)

How can we choose prepositions to make our sentences more specific? The following sentences might all be true, but which one of them is most precise?

- The person was with the car.
- The person was near the car.
- The person was behind the car.

Skills Covered in this Lesson

- Use knowledge of language and its conventions when writing, speaking, reading or listening.

Teacher Tip!

You could give the students a two-column graphic organizer to document the sentences. The first column would prompt the students to record their sentences. The second column would prompt the students to identify and list the prepositions that the students used.

Common Prepositions

aboard	about	above	across	after
against	along	amid	among	anti
around	as	at	before	behind
below	beneath	beside	besides	between
beyond	but	by	concerning	considering
despite	down	during	except	excepting
excluding	following	for	from	in
inside	intro	like	minus	near
of	off	on	onto	opposite
outside	over	past	per	plus
regarding	round	save	since	than
through	to	toward	towards	under
underneath	unlike	until	up	upon
versus	via	with	within	without

Figure 24.1

Lesson Twenty-Five

Prefix Carousel

Overview and Tips for Classroom Implementation

This mini lesson is designed for students to become more familiar with prefix meanings. This lesson also gives students the opportunity to brainstorm and think about word creation.

Lesson Instructions

Before beginning the activity, look at Figure 25.2 and choose the prefixes you want students to work on. Create a poster for each prefix by writing the prefix, meaning, and example on each poster board. For a class of about twenty-five students, plan to have at least ten prefix poster boards.

First, post the prefix poster boards around the classroom. Divide the students into groups of three.

Next, instruct the student groups that they are to walk around the room to visit each station. They'll be going in a circle, like a carousel. When a group arrives at a poster, they'll have 30 seconds to write down as many words that they can think of, using the prefix listed on the poster board. It is helpful to use a timer to keep students on task and focused. When the thirty seconds are up, students will move to the next poster board.

Then, when they arrive at a new poster board, direct the students to look at the words on the new poster board and add to the previous group's list. Give the students thirty seconds to add more words to the poster.

Continue until all student groups have visited all prefix posters and contributed to each list.

Skills Covered in this Lesson

- Demonstrate command of the conventions of standard English grammar and usage when writing or speaking.

Teacher Tip!

When the students are working on the last four or five prefix poster boards, I allow them to use dictionaries because it becomes increasingly challenging to generate more words for the lists. It is also helpful to increase the time at each station as the students progress through the groups.

Figure 25.1

Commonly Used Prefixes

Prefix	Meaning	Word Examples
anti	against	antifreeze
de	opposite	defrost
dis	not, opposite of	disembark
en, em	cause to	enforce, embrace
in, im	in	infield
in, im	not	injustice, impossible
inter	between	interplay
mid	middle	midway
mis	wrongly	misinform
non	not	nonsense
over	over	overpass
pre	before	prefix, preview
re	again	rerun
semi	half	semitransparent
sub	under	subway
super	above	supernova
trans	across	transport
un	not	unfriendly

Figure 25.2

Lesson Twenty-Six

Prefix Puzzle

Overview and Tips for Classroom Implementation

This mini lesson is intended to develop students' understanding of prefixes.

Lesson Instructions

First, prior to the lesson, you will need enough copies of the prefix graphic organizer (see Figure 26.1) for each group of students, and five different colors of construction paper. Each prefix group should be a different color, with the puzzle pieces either photocopied or written onto them.

Group 1: Copy onto blue paper the puzzle pieces with divided words to demonstrate the prefix *sub*.

sub	way
sub	marine

Group 2: Copy onto red paper the puzzle pieces with divided words to demonstrate the prefix *pre*.

pre	view
pre	sent

Group 3: Copy onto green paper the puzzle pieces with divided words to demonstrate the prefix *mis*.

mis   take
mis   understand

Group 4: Copy onto yellow paper the puzzle pieces with divided words to demonstrate the prefix *inter*.

inter   play
inter   view

Next, divide the class into groups of three students. Give each group all of the prefix puzzle pieces and a copy of the prefix graphic organizer.

Then, instruct the students to put the puzzle pieces together, matching the divided words. Once the students have correctly assembled the puzzle pieces, they can complete the prefix graphic organizer (see Figure 21).

Skills Covered in this Lesson

- Demonstrate command of the conventions of standard English grammar and usage when writing or speaking.

Teacher Tip!

Once the students have completed the prefix graphic organizer, I like to have a large group discussion about the words. I ask the students if they notice any patterns and what they may have learned about the different prefixes. We make a chart together, recording what they have learned about prefixes and any additional observations that they made about the language.

Prefix Graphic Organizer

Name:

Date:

Prefix	Prefix Meaning	Words	More words with the same prefix
sub			
pre			
mis			
inter			

Figure 26.1

Lesson Twenty-Seven

Pronoun Practice

Overview and Tips for Classroom Implementation

Students often forget to identify the antecedent when using pronouns in writing. As a result, the reader can become confused when the pronoun does not have an easily understood referent.

Lesson Instructions

First, review with students the relationship between pronouns and antecedents.

Each pronoun takes the place of a noun and refers to the noun which it replaces. The correct pronouns must be used so that the reader clearly understands which noun your pronoun is referring to.

Next, make copies of the Pronoun Practice worksheet (see Figure 27.1). The students can work in pairs or small groups, or the class can work through the activity as a whole-group instruction.

Then, have the students read one of the passages on the Pronoun Practice worksheet. They will notice that pronouns are missing. Instruct the students to insert appropriate pronouns where they are missing. Once the pronouns are inserted, instruct the students to identify the antecedent for each pronoun.

Finally, have the students take turns reading their completed passage aloud while another student pantomimes or "acts out" the action described in the passage. If the choice of pronoun makes the action unclear, let the students stop and correct it.

Repeat the activity with all four passages.

Skills Covered in this Lesson

- Demonstrate command of the conventions of standard English grammar and usage when writing or speaking.

Teacher Tips!

1. It is helpful to color-code the pronouns and the antecedent so that these are more obvious to the students.

2. As extra support, you may want to hand out or post a Pronoun Word Bank so students can refer to it during the activity.

    Pronoun Word Bank:
    she/her/hers/herself
    he/him/his/himself
    it/it/its/itself
    they/them/their/themselves

Overview and Tips for Classroom Implementation

My students were always surprised when I explained how gender pronouns functioned in Standard English. This mini lesson is designed to increase student awareness of gender and language through the study of pronouns.

Lesson Instructions

First, have the students select a character from this list: *cowboy, teacher, rock star, nurse, doctor,* or *lawyer*. Once the students have selected a character, give them twenty minutes to draft a one-to-two paragraph narrative story about the selected character using the Pronouns - Gender Impact handout (see Figure 28.2).

Next, divide the students into pairs. Instruct the students to circle the pronouns that their partner used to describe the selected character. Ask the students to answer the following questions:

> What is the gender of the character?
>
> How do you know the gender of the character (indicated by what pronouns were assigned)?

Then, allow a few minutes for each student to draw a quick sketch of their partner's character.

Next, have students take turns reading their partner's story aloud, pointing to the sketch every time they say the character's name or personal pronoun.

Finally, ask the students to share the answers to the questions in Step Two as part of a large group discussion. Discuss with the students how pronouns can impact the reader's assumptions about a text. The students can use the Pronouns - Gender Impact graphic organizer (see Figure 28.3) with characters and tally the gender assignments.

Skills Covered in this Lesson

- Demonstrate command of the conventions of standard English grammar and usage when writing or speaking.

Teacher Tip!

Teachers should respect district policy and community norms when deciding whether or not to include non-binary pronouns such as the singular they/them/their in this activity. As of this writing, the SAT and ACT tests recognize only he/him/his and she/her/hers as singular, personal pronouns. The following resource offers tips for avoiding gender-biased language in writing:

owl.purdue.edu/owl/general_writing/grammar/pronouns/gendered_pronouns_and_singular_they.html

Student Sample: Pronouns – Gender Impact

Character: Rock star

Story: Geraldine is a serious rock star. She is in a band that plays punk rock music. She plays the guitar, bass and drums. Sometimes Geraldine sings, and Tommy or George take turns on bass and guitar. Geraldine is the only drummer in the band. The band plays lots of shows. They will play anywhere for anyone who wants to see them. Geraldine is in charge of booking and promotions. She is the most organized member of the band, although all of the band members are equally committed. When Geraldine graduates from school, she hopes to be able to play music all the time as her job. Geraldine has wanted to be a musician since kindergarten.

Character	Pronouns Associated with the Character	Female or Male?
cowboy	he, him, she	both
teacher	he, she	both
rock star	he, she, him, her, they	both
nurse	he, she, him, her, they	both
doctor	she, he, her, him, they	both
lawyer	she, he, her, him, they	both

Figure 28.1

Pronouns – Gender Impact

Name:

Date:

Character: _____

Story: _____

_____

_____

_____

_____

_____

_____

_____

_____

_____

_____

Figure 28.2

Pronouns – Gender Impact

Name:

Date:

Character	Pronouns Associated with the Character	Female or Male?
cowboy		
teacher		
rock star		
nurse		
doctor		
lawyer		

Figure 28.3

Lesson Twenty-Nine

Pronouns: Possessive

Overview and Tips for Classroom Implementations

A pronoun used to demonstrate possession is called a possessive pronoun. Students are often confused when to use the masculine, feminine, or neuter form of possessive. This lesson allows students to practice with the different possessive pronouns.

Lesson Instructions

First, review the possessive pronouns with the students:

mine, yours, his, hers, its, ours, yours, and *theirs*

As illustrated in the following examples, possessive pronouns demonstrate relationships.

It is *mine*.
First person pronoun, *mine*, refers to the speaker.

No, it is not *yours*.
Second person pronoun, *yours*, refers to the person being spoken to (you).

Maybe it is *hers*.
Third person pronoun, *hers*, refers to the person being spoken about (she).

I know *its* shape seems odd.
Third person pronoun, *its*, refers to an object, not a person.

Next, once you have reviewed possessive pronouns with the students, ask the students to create sentences like those in your examples. The students can work in pairs to create the sentences. It should take about five minutes to create sample sentences for each of the possessive pronouns.

Then, instruct the students to select three of the sample sentences that they created. Next, the students will illustrate the relationship of each possessive pronoun. Give the students about ten minutes to complete these steps.

Skills Covered in this Lesson

- Demonstrate command of the conventions of standard English grammar and usage when writing or speaking.

Teacher Tips!

1. If you have access to computers in your classroom, use a drawing program for the students to create the possessive pronoun.
2. When the students illustrate the possessive pronoun relationships, they can do so in a variety of formats. I have successfully used both of these methods:
   - Bring large butcher block paper and tape it to a wall in the classroom. The students stand and create their illustrations on the butcher block paper.
   - Distribute card stock and ask students to draw one sample possessive pronoun on each card.

Notes

Lesson Thirty

Proper Nouns

Overview and Tips for Classroom Implementation

Since there are several types of nouns, student writers need to understand how they differ. Student writers make frequent errors in capitalization that are often the result of not knowing and understanding what designates a proper noun. This lesson reviews the characteristics of proper nouns and provides practice for the students.

Lesson Instructions

First, obtain a box or large bag. Collect a variety of items that could be designated as a proper noun. For example, a map with the country, city, or location circled; pictures of famous people; photos of famous buildings; small toy cars; or excerpts from famous documents or texts. Put about twenty to thirty items in the bags.

Next, using Figure 30.1, review the characteristics of proper nouns and explain why these words are capitalized.

Then, circulate among the students and invite them to draw an item from the box or bag that you created. When a student takes out an item--let's say for this example that it's a map with a city circled--instruct the student to show the item to the class.

Finally, the students should identify the proper noun (in this example, it's the name of a city) and explain why it is a proper noun and should be capitalized. Repeat this procedure until the items have all been selected.

Skills Covered in this Lesson

- Demonstrate command of the conventions of standard English grammar and usage when writing or speaking.
- Demonstrate command of the conventions of standard English capitalization, punctuation, and spelling when writing.

Teacher Tips!

1. Posting the list (Figure 30.1) supports visual learners and students who have challenges with processing.
2. Keep the rules and criteria for proper nouns posted as you and the students go through the items. The students can use the list (Figure 30.1) as a reference throughout the activity.

Proper Nouns

Proper nouns, like other nouns, name a person, place, thing or idea. However, proper nouns further distinguish nouns since they name or label a particular entity, unlike common nouns.

Proper nouns are capitalized.

Proper nouns are not usually preceded by an article (a, an, the).

Proper nouns name specific people, places, organizations and sometimes things.

Here are some examples:

Specific people and their titles:
- Nelson Mandela
- President Roosevelt
- Queen Elizabeth
- Mayor La Guardia
- Aunt Maria
- Ms. Harrison
- Dr. Valencia

Specific objects and buildings:
- Magna Carta
- The Liberty Bell
- Eiffel Tower
- Empire State Building
- Sydney Opera House

Specific places:
- Chicago
- Arizona
- Egypt
- Antarctica
- Pacific Ocean
- Mount Everest
- Fifth Avenue
- Grand Canyon National Park
- The Liberty Bell
- Amazon River

Specific businesses and products:
- Google
- American Airlines
- McDonald's
- Nike
- Cheerios
- Animal Crossing
- Ford F-150
- Chromebook

Figure 30.1

Lesson Thirty-One

Quotation Marks, Part One

Overview and Tips for Classroom Implementation

There are many rules which students must know and remember when using quotations in writing. The next group of lessons examines how quotation marks are used in a variety of circumstances.

Lesson Instructions

Before beginning, create envelopes with copies of preselected titles written on slips of paper.

First, because students are often confused about when to underline/italicize titles and when to use quotation marks, I begin this lesson by explaining the rules. Titles are put in quotation marks when they are part of a larger work. For example, articles are part of newspapers or magazines. Poems and essays are usually part of a larger volume of collected poems and essays. Song titles are usually part of an artist's album or playlist. That's why they are punctuated with quotation marks. Titles of books, movies, plays, music albums, websites, newspapers and magazines are stand-alone and are underlined/italicized.

Next, divide the students into groups of three or four. Instruct them to examine the titles from their envelopes and sort them into categories: underline/italicize or punctuate with quotation marks. Give them about five minutes to complete this activity. Display a timer to support student focus.

Then, once the students have determined how a title should be punctuated, review the responses with the students as a large-group activity.

Skills Covered in this Lesson

- Demonstrate command of the conventions of standard English capitalization, punctuation, and spelling when writing.

Teacher Tips!

1. You may need to also explain that, while italicizing is easy on the computer, it's difficult to do when writing by hand. In such cases, underlining is still used and is the same as writing a title in italics. It is never correct to both italicize and underline a title, though!
2. For further practice and assessment, invite the students to create lists of titles that their classmates can punctuate.

Standards/Skills Based Grading

Jump-start & create a positive assessment culture!

Contact us at
info@EngagingLearners.com
or call **(312) 576-8222**

to schedule a free, no-obligation phone consultation with Dr. McKnight

The Engaging Learners team can come to YOU!

Traditional A, B, C, D, F grading is woefully inadequate in today's K-12 learning environment. Standards/Skills-Based Grading (SBG) incorporates research-based practices like descriptive feedback and formative assessment that complement Social Emotional Learning (SEL) standards. Together, they prepare all students for success in school and in life.

Transitioning between paradigms is challenging work. We can help.

Lesson Thirty-Two

Quotation Marks, Part Two

Overview and Tips for Classroom Implementation

This mini lesson will focus on the situations in which quotation marks are needed. The students will work in collaborative groups to identify and list the reasons for using quotation marks in writing.

Lesson Instructions

First, before beginning the activity, tape signs to the classroom walls that say:

- exact words someone else has written
- exact words someone else has spoken
- words as words
- alternate meaning or sarcasm

Next, introduce quotation marks and discuss the following examples. Be sure to explain how open and closed quotation marks indicate the beginning and end of the actual words of a speaker or writer, or the beginning and end of the word or phrase that is being referred to.

Quotation Examples:

1. Reason for Quotation: repeating **exact words someone else has *written*.**

Example: The columnist wrote in the school newspaper, "If the school administration is truly concerned about student health and obesity, better food that is not heavily processed must be served."

2. Reason for Quotation: repeating **exact words someone else has *spoken.***
   Example: When Jenna interviewed Principal Smith she asked him, "What efforts have been made to improve the quality of school cafeteria food?"

3. Reason for Quotation: to talk about **words as words.**
   Examples: Ellie's favorite adjective is "compassionate."
   "Circulate freely" means to move continuously without restrictions.

4. Reason for Quotation: to imply **alternate meaning or sarcasm.**
   Examples: Duncan could see the "surprise" coming from a mile away.
   I paid extra for the "premium" version, but I couldn't even get it to start.

Next, once you have reviewed the examples and reasons for quotation marks, divide the students into groups of three or four members. Instruct the groups to write one or two examples for each of the four "Reasons for Quotation" on index cards or small pieces of paper.

Then, instruct the students to exchange their sentences with another group. Once the students have received the sentences from another group, instruct them to identify the "Reasons for Quotation" and ask them to tape or hang the sentences under the appropriate "Reason for Quotation" sign.

Finally, discuss the sentences as a full class activity. Invite the class to make suggestions and edits if necessary, and rearrange the student sentences so that they're all identified correctly.

Skills Covered in this Lesson

- Demonstrate command of the conventions of standard English grammar and usage when writing or speaking.

Teacher Tips!

1. If you want to create a slightly less physical activity, use a 4-column graphic organizer with each "Reason for Quotation" as the header for each column. The students can record the sentences that they received from the other group under the appropriate header in the graphic organizer rather than hanging sentences on the walls.

2. Don't be surprised if students have a difficult time writing sentences that use quotation marks to indicate alternate meaning or sarcasm. This is a particularly difficult concept and isn't encountered very often in academic writing. You may want to use "air quotes" as a way to explain the concept. Speakers sometimes use air quote gestures in casual conversation, combined with tone and expression, to indicate that they don't agree with a word choice. Here are two videos that explain it:

SPOOKY Scare Quotes [SAT/ACT Reading] by Brilliant Prep
youtube.com/watch?v=-Y_cE9rnLZI

What exactly are "AIR QUOTES"? by Eringlish
youtube.com/watch?v=9unTPt51ILo

Lesson Thirty-Three

Semicolon

Overview and Tips for Classroom Implementation

Most student writers do not use the semicolon, largely because they don't have enough experience with this punctuation mark. In this lesson, students will examine how written language relates to spoken language. Students will explore the use of the semicolon as they compare written speeches and their verbal deliveries. Looking at real-world examples by respected orators is an effective method for explaining the two purposes of the semicolon.

Lesson Instructions

First, before beginning this activity, find a few strong examples of semicolon usage. You'll need excerpts from written speeches and their corresponding recording. A few suggestions are:

"Wellesley High School Commencement Address" by David McCullough, Jr.: americanrhetoric.com/speeches/davidmcculloughwellesleyhighschoolcommencement.htm

"A Whisper of AIDS: 1992 Republican National Convention Address" by Mary Fisher: americanrhetoric.com/speeches/maryfisher1992rnc.html

"Women's Rights are Human Rights" by Hillary Rodham Clinton: americanrhetoric.com/speechbank.htm

"A Plea for Mercy" by Clarence Darrow: americanrhetoric.com/speeches/cdarrowpleaformercy.htm

Next, review the correct usage of the semicolon. Explain how it is used sparingly in academic writing (1) to separate items in a series or list, and (2) to connect two closely related sentences in order to emphasize their relationship. In this activity, students will be focusing on the second usage.

Then, model the activity for the full class by comparing a written excerpt with its spoken recording. Circle the sentence with the semicolon. Listen to the recording and discuss how the speaker's delivery reflects the punctuation.

Next, practice rewriting the circled sentence as two shorter sentences, adding a conjunction if necessary. Brainstorm all the ways the original sentence could be rewritten.

Then, invite students to read the original sentence and all the rewritten versions aloud. Discuss the subtle differences. In the original speech, did the writer's use of a semicolon prompt the speaker focus on the connection between the two ideas? Give students an opportunity to say all the versions aloud. Can they hear the difference between connected ideas and distinct ideas? Can they create that subtle distinction with their own speech? Why may the author of the original speech have chosen to use a semicolon instead of writing one of the two-sentence versions you thought of.

Finally, divide the students up into groups of 2-4 students. Ask them to repeat the activity using excerpts from other speeches. They should record their work in the Semicolons graphic organizer (Figure 33.1).

Skills Covered in this Lesson

- Demonstrate command of the conventions of standard English grammar and usage when writing or speaking.
- Evaluate a speaker's point of view, reasoning, and use of evidence and rhetoric.
- Integrate and evaluate information presented in diverse media and formats, including visually, quantitatively, and orally.

Teacher Tips!

1. The American Rhetoric speech bank is a good place to look for recordings and transcripts of speeches. Proofread them first. You'll want to determine if they're good examples of semicolon usage and confirm that they are appropriate for your students.

americanrhetoric.com/speechbank.htm

2. Unless you're working with text that students are familiar with, it helps to provide some context for the quote.
3. This lesson is a good companion to the Connecting Clauses lesson.

Semicolons Graphic Organizer

Name:

Date:

Passage That Contains a Semicolon	Rewrite the passage as two or more shorter sentences.	How does the semicolon affect how you read the passage?

Figure 33.1

Notes

Lesson Thirty-Four

Sentence Fragments

Overview and Tips for Classroom Implementation

This lesson is designed to give students practice in identifying sentence fragments. Sentence fragments and sentence run-ons are difficult for students to understand because they require writers to apply everything that they know and understand about grammar and sentence structure.

Lesson Instructions

First, prior to conducting the lesson in class, print enough copies of Figure 34.1 for each group of students. I suggest having the students work in pairs or in groups of no more than four students. Cut out the sentence fragment strips from Figure 34.1 and place them in an envelope for each group.

Next, model the activity by discussing some sentence fragments and brainstorming answers to the following questions:

> What makes a sentence fragment a sentence fragment? As you look at the sample sentence fragments, ask yourself, what's missing? What information do I need after reading this sentence fragment? What information can I add to create a sentence that has a complete meaning?
>
> **Tip:** You might want to point out that sentence fragments are ineffective writing because they create confusion for the reader.

Then, divide the students into pairs or groups of no more than four students. Distribute the sentence strip envelopes that were cut out from Figure 34.1. Direct the students to do the following:

1. Take the strips out of the envelope.
2. Combine two strips to create a complete sentence.
3. Add punctuation and capitalization to form a complete sentence.

Finally, once the students have created the completed sentences, they can submit them for evaluation. The students can also share their sentences as a whole group. Whichever method you choose, discuss how the students revised the strips to create complete, coherent sentences.

Skills Covered in this Lesson

- Demonstrate command of the conventions of standard English capitalization, punctuation, and spelling when writing.

Teacher Tips!

1. The students can record the sentences that they create and discuss them as a whole group.
2. The students can create sentence fragment strips for another round of practice. These newly created sentence fragment strips can be exchanged with other student groups.

Sentence Fragment Strips

I wonder if Duncan

would let me use his basketball

my grandmother loves to tell me

stories about her life on the farm

her little sister likes

to play with dolls nearly every day

would someone please make

a chocolate cake for my birthday

my favorite music is

featured on this website

Janis doesn't

care if the party is canceled

that class has a clever way

of deciding what book to read next

Figure 34.1

Lesson Thirty-Five
Spelling Words That Challenge Us

Overview and Tips for Classroom Implementation

Despite spell-check, there are words that are challenging for students to spell correctly. This lesson provides practice for students to spell some of the most challenging words.

Lesson Instructions

First, prior to the lesson, make a copy of Figure 35.1 for the students.

Next, distribute Figure 35.1 to the students and instruct them to identify which words are tricky to spell. Have the students record the tricky words in the Personal Spelling Dictionary graphic organizer (Figure 35.3).

Then, divide the students up into pairs or small groups. Instruct them to brainstorm memory tricks or strategies to help them remember how to spell their tricky words. There are lots of mnemonic devices to try. Encourage students to consider:

1. drawing pictures, looking for words embedded in the tricky word (For example: PIEce of PIE);

2. physically representing words (For example: spell c-o-l-u-m-N while drawing a tall letter "N" in the air to represent a column; or act out student drivers, scratching their heads while they take the test to get a driver's LICEnse.); or

3. creating phrases using the letters of a word (embaRRaSSed = he got Really Red when his Sister Sang).

Skills Covered in this Lesson

- Demonstrate command of the conventions of standard English capitalization, punctuation, and spelling when writing.

Teacher Tips!

1. Once the students start this personal spelling list, they can continue to add to it throughout the school year.
2. Be prepared to model this activity and provide examples.
3. Don't be tempted to have students do this activity independently. Students really benefit from working with peers to come up with unique mnemonic devices, and they're more likely to retain their "memory tricks."

Words That Are Tricky to Spell

absence	defendant	height	manipulate	sergeant
accidentally	definite	heiress	mileage	sizable
acquaint	dilemma	heredity	minuscule	success
acquire	discipline	humane	misspell	suspicion
aerial	eighth	icicle	neighbor	symmetry
analysis	emigrate	ideally	niceties	tendency
analyze	emphasis	immature	nickel	thorough
apparent	exceed	immigrate	niece	through
appearance	excessive	interfere	nominal	thwart
belief	existence	interrupt	nonentity	tonal
believe	flabbergast	irregular	occurred	tragedy
bureau	fractious	jaunty	occurrence	truly
calendar	gauge	jealous	omnipotent	unified
catastrophe	genuine	justification	operable	unique
category	grateful	knowledge	paradigm	unnecessary
cemetery	gratitude	liberal	persuasive	usually
changeable	grisly	license	possess	vicious
column	guarantee	likelihood	regrettable	villain
committed	guilty	lonely	reliance	violin
condemn	handkerchief	loveable	rhythm	weird
conscience	handsome	luxury	secede	wield
conscious	handedly	mammoth	seize	yield
courageous	handwritten	manageable	separate	zealous

Figure 35.1

Student Sample: Personal Spelling Dictionary

Word List	How Can I Remember to Spell It
chocolate	I eat chocolate late at night, "choco-late".
paradigm	Paradigm looks silly, like "Para dig em!"
artistic	Artistic, 'art', 'is', 'tic'.
basketball	Basketball is like a basket of balls.
Mississippi	Double double 's', single double 'p'.
catalog	Catalog, a cat on a log.
icicle	icicle (drawn as icicles with drips)
handkerchief	The fire CHIEF held a HANDkerCHIEF in his HAND.
believe	I beliEVE in EVE.

Figure 35.2

Personal Spelling Dictionary

Name:

Date:

Word List	How Can I Remember to Spell It

Figure 35.3

Lesson Thirty-Six

Subject and Verb Agreement

Overview and Tips for Classroom Implementation

We learn grammar best through authentic language experiences. In this lesson, students will explore authentic texts such as song lyrics and newspapers, and identify correct and incorrect uses and examples of subject and verb agreement. There are three variations of this activity. Feel free to use one or all of them in your classroom.

Lesson Instructions

First, review subject-verb agreement. Discuss how subject-verb agreement changes in various forms of written text and the effect that it has on the content.

Next, instruct the students to go to the website of a local newspaper and have them select two to three headlines that grab their attention. Instruct the students to find the subject and verb in each headline. The students might have some difficulty finding the subject and verb and determining if there is agreement in the headline. If they do, be sure to discuss and assist the students.

Then, invite students to take turns reading the headlines aloud, using their best newscaster voice. When the reading is over, other students can repeat the subject and verb together. For example, one student reads the headline,

"Mayor Announces New Parking Restrictions." The class responds with, "Mayor announces."

Next, select several examples of dialogue from a variety of novels, plays or short stories. Distribute the sentence samples and instruct the students to identify the subject and verb. Have the students determine if the subject and verb in each sentence agrees.

Then, invite students to read the lines of dialogue aloud. Some students may want to "act" or use funny voices and that's fine! Remember, playing with language and grammar helps students get comfortable with it.

Finally, repeat the activity with song lyrics. Write a selection of lyrics from popular songs on index cards or slips of paper. Invite students to choose a few favorites. After identifying the subject-verb agreement, let the class speak or sing the lyric while clapping on the subject and verb. For example, they'll sing "I hit the road in overdrive" while clapping on the words "I" and "hit."

Skills Covered in this Lesson

- Demonstrate command of the conventions of standard English capitalization, punctuation, and spelling when writing.
- Use knowledge of language and its conventions when writing, speaking, reading or listening.

Teacher Tips!

1. Be sure that students work with examples in which the subject and verb agree. Popular songs and fictional dialogue sometimes include deliberate mistakes. Avoid reinforcing incorrect usage.
2. The activities in this lesson work as whole class activities but some teachers prefer to divide their students into small groups or pairs.
3. Once the students have identified subjects and verbs in a variety of texts and determined whether there is agreement, have them take a practice quiz.

Literacy & Learning Centers™

Close the achievement gap with interactive, collaborative learning!

Dr. Katherine McKnight has a 100% success rate in achieving academic gains with her unique, centers-based approach – designed specifically for grade 4-12 learners.

> ## Contact us at
> ## info@EngagingLearners.com
> ## or call **(312) 576-8222**
>
> to schedule a free, no-obligation phone consultation with Dr. McKnight

Every teacher, in every school and every class, can enjoy huge growth in student proficiency while creating a collaborative learning environment. Join hundreds of schools all across the country by incorporating this research-based model.

Read the book, take the on-demand course, visit the website, watch the video, or invite Dr. Katherine McKnight to lead professional development in your school.

Use the Literacy & Learning Center model to teach content *and* develop literacy!

Lesson Thirty-Seven

Writer's Proofreading Checklist

Overview and Tips for Classroom Implementation

Student writers need tools that support them to evaluate and proofread their own writing. This lesson incorporates a graphic organizer that student writers can use to proofread.

Lesson Instructions

Before beginning this lesson, make enough copies of the Writer's Proofreading Handout (see Figure 37.1), Proofreading Practice Slips (see Figure 37.2), and the Writer's Proofreading Checklist (see Figure 37.3).

First, remind your students about the importance of proofreading. I always explain to my students that word processing programs do not catch every error. I also remind them that, in addition to checking grammar, spelling, and punctuation, they also proofread to make sure their writing is coherent and understandable.

Next, review the Proofreading Handout together. Explain that some of these examples aren't grammatically incorrect; rather, they are a matter of style. Different forms of writing require different styles. For example, writing in second-person or using slang would be appropriate in a friendly letter or email, but they are to be avoided in academic writing.

Then, cut up the Proofreading Practice Slips (see Figure 37.2). Give students an opportunity to recognize examples of these errors by sorting the 12 sentence slips into the 6 proofreading categories: Verb Tense, Passive Voice, Third Person, Slang and Colloquialisms, Filler Words and Phrases, and Tricky Words and Phrases. Students can complete this activity individually or work in pairs. When the activity is complete, review and discuss the results.

Finally, give students a copy of the Writer's Proofreading Checklist (see Figure 37.3). Let them proofread one of their own pieces of writing, paying particular attention to the 6 proofreading categories that have been reviewed in this lesson. Not every student will find examples of every mistake. Encourage them to write comments to document what they found and how they rewrote it.

Skills Covered in this Lesson

- Demonstrate command of the conventions of standard English grammar and usage when writing or speaking.
- Demonstrate command of the conventions of standard English capitalization, punctuation, and spelling when writing.
- Use knowledge of language and its conventions when writing, speaking, reading or listening.
- Respond to the varying demands of audience, task, purpose, and discipline.

Teacher Tips!

1. This activity can be adapted to support proofreading for any grammatical challenge! Create your own checklists and handouts to include concepts like sentence fragments, subject-verb agreement, comma usage, end punctuation, etc. Limit the sorting activity to six or fewer categories each time to avoid overwhelming students.
2. Have the students keep a copy of the handout in their notebook or folder.
3. Provide copies of the checklist for students to use whenever they proofread, or encourage them to make their own checklists.

Writer's Proofreading Handout

Verb Tense should be used logically and consistently. Don't shift between past tense, present, and future tense unless there is a passage of time. *If you switch tense, is there a good reason?*
> Avoid inconsistent verb tense like this:
> It was quiet in the locker room and there isn't any celebration.

Passive Voice describes a style of writing that uses a form of the verb *to be* (examples: *is, was, were, has been, will be,* etc.) and is usually vaguely informative. Writing in the passive voice isn't incorrect; it's just not very precise. *Look for the verb "to be" and decide if you'd rather use the active voice to express your meaning.*
> Avoid using passive voice like this:
> That day was never forgotten by the students.

Third Person point of view is best for academic writing. When you write in third-person you don't use *I* or *we* as a subject and you don't refer to the reader as *you*. That's called second person point of view and it's rarely acceptable in academic writing. *Avoid using "I," "we," "you," and "us," unless you're writing informally, quoting someone or telling a personal story.*
> Avoid writing from second person point of view like this:
> I'll explain my ideas so you will understand my reasoning.

Slang and Colloquialisms should be avoided in academic writing because a reader who is unfamiliar with these phrases may be confused. *Ask yourself if someone 40 years older than you, living on the other side of the country, would understand your meaning.*
> Avoid using slang or colloquialisms like this:
> When Brendan got the award he flexed for forty minutes straight.

Filler Words and Phrases like *totally, like, basically, I mean,* and *you know,* should be avoided in academic writing. *Do all words and phrases affect the meaning of the sentence? If not, consider eliminating them.*
> Avoid using filler words and phrases like this:
> Iwo Jima is basically one of the most famous battles from World War II.

Tricky Words and Phrases are different for every writer. Consider commonly confused word pairs like *its-it's, whose-who's, affect-effect, accept-except,* and *led-lead;* and think about easily misspelled words. *What words are tricky for you? Look for them during proofreading and always double-check them.*
> Look for tricky words and phrases; they might be wrong like this:
> Denise put the equipment back in it's case.

Figure 37.1

Proofreading Practice Slips

Verb Tense	Passive
Third Person	Slang and Colloquialisms
Filler Words and Phrases	Tricky Words and Phrases

By early evening the storm clouds cleared and the rain finally stops.

On Wednesday he gives the little girl crayons but did not let her paint.

The lunches will be delivered by Terri's dad.

The antelope was chased by the lion.

You probably thought the same thing yourself.

We can now consider the next example.

Her mother said not to but Saundra lowkey went to the party anyway.

The new pianist slayed her solo at the winter concert.

Ted is like the highest scoring player to ever play for the Highland Hawks.

The old tomcat totally enjoyed sleeping on the armchair.

Maurice ate all the jellybeans accept for the cinnamon ones.

The coach lost count and didn't know who's turn came next.

Figure 37.2

Writer's Proofreading Checklist

Name:

Title of Piece:

Date:

Proofreading Reminder	I checked for this.	Comments
Verb Tense should be used logically and consistently.		
Passive Voice describes a style of writing that uses a form of the verb *to be* (examples: *is, was, were, has been, will be,* etc.) and is usually vaguely informative.		
Third Person point of view is best for academic writing.		
Slang and Colloquialisms should be avoided in academic writing because a reader who is unfamiliar with these phrases may be confused.		
Filler Words and Phrases like *totally, like, basically, I mean,* and *you know,* should be avoided in academic writing.		
Tricky Words and Phrases are different for every writer. Consider commonly confused word pairs like its-it's, whose-who's, affect-effect, accept-except, and led-lead; and easily misspelled words.		

Figure 37.3

Lesson Thirty-Eight

Very

Overview and Tips for Classroom Implementation

I developed this lesson when it seemed to me that every student in my classes used the word "very" at least ten times in every written assignment. This activity will encourage students to reflect on the overuse of the word. It will also provide them with a list of synonyms for "very" that they can use on those occasions when they believe an intensifier is necessary.

Lesson Instructions

Before beginning this lesson, make enough copies of the Very - Synonym Worksheet Slips (Figure 38.1) and the Very Handout (Figure 38.2). You can cut out the slips and put them in envelopes for the students or they can do that step themselves.

First, explain to the students that the word "very" is overused and should be avoided in our writing. Invite them to reflect on the impulse to use intensifiers like "very". Do they not trust their word choice, and are they searching for a stronger way to express their idea? Remind them that they can use a thesaurus to help them find alternatives. If they can't find a perfect alternative and they still want to use an intensifier, explain that there are also synonyms for the word "very". They should consider using one of those.

Then, give students the Very - Synonym Worksheet Slips. Invite them to sort out the Very Expressions from the Very Synonyms.

Next, ask students to choose a Very Expression. Tell them to take a blank slip and cover up the word "very". How does that affect the expression? It's possible that an intensifier isn't needed.

Then, tell them to choose a few Very Synonym Slips and replace the word "very". How do these intensifiers change the sense of the expression? Did they learn any new intensifiers? Which ones are their favorites?

Next, have them repeat the activity, exploring different Very Synonyms for each expression.

Finally, hand out copies of the Very Handout. Ask them to circle their synonyms that are new to them. Invite them to keep the handout in their writing notebook or folder.

Skills Covered in this Lesson

- Demonstrate command of the conventions of standard English grammar and usage when writing or speaking.
- Analyze how specific word choices shape meaning or tone.

Teacher Tip!

The students can create additional "very" expressions and create quizzes for each other for additional practice.

Very – Synonym Worksheet Slips

Very Expressions	Very Synonyms
very painful	agonizingly
very stormy	awfully
very happy	certainly
very lonely	extremely
very sad	greatly
very indifferent	incredibly
very knowledgeable	quite
very dry	really
very wet	surprisingly
very soon	terribly
very often	thoroughly
very infrequent	too
very hopeless	truly
very sweet	unusually
very salty	utterly
very clear	wonderfully

Figure 38.1

Very Handout

The word "very" is overused. It doesn't add much to a sentence and it is annoying to readers and listeners. What can you do?

Find a word that is strong enough on its own so you don't need an intensifier, or use one of these words instead!

absolutely	greatly	simply
actually	highly	strikingly
acutely	hugely	substantially
awfully	immensely	surprisingly
certainly	incredibly	terribly
completely	notably	thoroughly
deeply	particularly	too
enormously	quite	tremendously
extensively	rather	truly
extremely	really	unusually
extraordinarily	seriously	utterly
genuinely	severely	wonderfully

Can you think of other words you might use in place of "very"? Write them here:

_____

_____

Finally, be careful you don't overuse one of these synonyms in place of "very" because that could be just as annoying.

Figure 38.2

Notes

Lesson Thirty-Nine

Words That Are Confusing

Overview and Tips for Classroom Implementation

Words can be confusing for different reasons. Sometimes they sound alike, and sometimes their pronunciation is different but their spelling is almost identical. Whatever the reason, English language learners and native speakers alike need extra practice with these confusing word pairs.

Lesson Instructions

Prior to the lesson, write each word of the Confusing Word Pairs on separate index cards (see Figure 39.1). You should have one card per student.

First, pass out cards to the students as they enter class. Once each student has one of the Confusing Word cards, instruct them to find the student with the matching word. For example, the student with "board" written on their card needs to find the student with "bored" because those two words sound alike. The student with "then" on their card needs to find the student with the word "than." Although those words don't sound exactly alike, they are often confused in both writing and speaking.

Next, once the students find their Confusing Word Pair partner, ask them to work together to provide brief explanations of their words. They should be able to explain what each word means and why it is different from its confusing partner word. Allow them to use dictionaries, glossaries or other resources if necessary.

Finally, when all pairs have finished, have them share their work with the full class.

Skills Covered in this Lesson

- Demonstrate command of the conventions of standard English grammar and usage when writing or speaking.

Teacher Tips!

1. As an extension activity, I like to have the students create posters that explain how the confusing words are different. The students also provide pictures, drawings, and cartoons to visualize the difference between the words.

2. If you'd like, add some 3-word groups to this activity. Two-too-to, their-there-they're, sight-cite-site, threw-through- though, and wear-where-were are good examples of confusing words that come in groups of three.

Confusing Word Pairs

accept except	board bored
brake break	capital capitol
choose chose	desert dessert
formally formerly	hear here
its it's	loose lose
quiet quite	peace piece
plain plane	principal principle
theirs there's	threw through
waist waste	weather whether
who's whose	your you're

Figure 39.1

Lesson Forty

Your and You're

Overview and Tips for Classroom Implementation

"Your" and "you're" are two of the most commonly confused words in the English language. This lesson reviews the meanings of "your" and "you're". The entertaining activity provides students an opportunity to practice recognizing the difference between the words.

Lesson Instructions

Prior to doing the lesson, print and cut apart copies of Your Bananas/You're Bananas (see Figure 40.1) so that each small group will have a set of cards. If you prefer, you can write these phrases on index cards. One card should say "your bananas". The other cards should say, "you're bananas".

First, show the students one of the following videos. They explain the difference between "your" (possessive) and "you're" (contraction of "you are"). Review the material as necessary.

"Your vs. You're Song" by Jonathan Mann
youtube.com/watch?v=DCc4PgF2Ris

"Difference Between Your and You're" by Editor OEE (Online English Editor)
youtube.com/watch?v=t0kFCzjJL9I

"Grammar: Your or You're?" by GCFLearnFree.org (Goodwill Community Foundation)
youtube.com/watch?v=pjAJswDB14s

Next, explain the meaning of the slang word "bananas." In addition to meaning a tropical fruit, it is also a slang word that can mean ridiculous, irrational, wildly enthusiastic, or in style.

> Examples: Sometimes TV for preschoolers is totally bananas.
> When I saw that mouse I went bananas for a minute.
> The crowd went bananas when the band came onstage.
> His new shoes were absolutely bananas.

Then, divide the class into small groups of 3-5 students. Give each group a set of index cards. Instruct students to take turns handing each other one card at a time.

If a student receives a "your bananas" card, they are supposed to reply, "Why thank you, I'll take them" and pantomime picking up a bunch of bananas. If the card says, "you're bananas" they should make a funny face, posture, or gesture to indicate that they are ridiculous, irrational, wildly enthusiastic, or fashionable.

Repeat the activity until everyone in the group has had a chance to pick up invisible bananas (your bananas) and make a funny face (you're bananas).

Skills Covered in this Lesson

- Demonstrate command of the conventions of standard English grammar and usage when writing or speaking.

Teacher Tips!

1. It's helpful if you model these reactions a few times yourself so students have a clear understanding of the level of volume and physicality that's permitted.
2. As always, when you plan to engage in a physical activity, review classroom norms with your students before starting.

Your Bananas / You're Bananas

your bananas

you're bananas

Figure 40.1

Made in United States
North Haven, CT
19 January 2022